DATE DUE

JA 9'06			
MY 12'06			
MY 19'06			
MR 13'06			
MR 16'07			

DEMCO NO. 38 - 2980

THE WAR
OF 1812

Titles in the American War Series

The American Revolution
"Give Me Liberty, or
Give Me Death!"
Paperback 0-7660-1727-3
Library Ed. 0-89490-521-X

The Civil War
"A House Divided"
Paperback 0-7660-1728-1
Library Ed. 0-89490-522-8

The Korean War
"The Forgotten War"
Paperback 0-7660-1729-X
Library Ed. 0-89490-526-0

The Mexican War
"Mr. Polk's War"
Library Ed. 0-7660-1853-9

The Persian Gulf War
"The Mother of All Battles"
Paperback 0-7660-1730-3
Library Ed. 0-89490-528-7

The Spanish-American War
"Remember the Maine!"
Library Ed. 0-7660-1855-5

The War of 1812
"We Have Met the Enemy and
They Are Ours"
Library Ed. 0-7660-1854-7

World War I
"The War to End Wars"
Paperback 0-7660-1732-X
Library Ed. 0-89490-523-6

World War II
in Europe
"America Goes to War"
Paperback 0-7660-1733-8
Library Ed. 0-89490-525-2

World War II
in the Pacific
"Remember Pearl Harbor"
Paperback 0-7660-1734-6
Library Ed. 0-89490-524-4

The Vietnam War
"What Are We Fighting For?"
Paperback 0-7660-1731-1
Library Ed. 0-89490-527-9

—American War Series—

THE WAR OF 1812

"We Have Met the Enemy and They Are Ours"

Karen Clemens Warrick

Enslow Publishers, Inc.

40 Industrial Road   PO Box 38
Box 398   Aldershot
Berkeley Heights, NJ 07922 Hants GU12 6BP
USA   UK

http://www.enslow.com

"We have met the enemy, and they are ours."

—Captain Oliver Hazard Perry's dispatch from the US brig *Niagara* to General William Henry Harrison announcing his victory at the Battle of Lake Erie on September 10, 1813

Library of Congress Cataloging-in-Publication Data

Warrick, Karen Clemens.
    The War of 1812 : "we have met the enemy and they are ours" / Karen Clemens Warrick.
        p. cm. — (American war series)
    Includes bibliographical references (p.) and index.
    Summary: Traces the history of the War of 1812, examining the maritime and boundary issues that caused it and highlighting the roles of famous personalities, including Oliver Hazard Perry, Andrew Jackson, and Dolley Madison.
    ISBN 0-7660-1854-7
        1. United States—History—War of 1812—Juvenile literature.
    [1.United States—History—War of 1812.] I. Title. II. Series.
    E354 .W39 2002
    973.5'2—dc21
                                                    2001004120

Printed in the United States of America

10 9 8 7 6 5 4 3 2 1

To Our Readers:
We have done our best to make sure all Internet Addresses in this book were active and appropriate when we went to press. However, the author and the publisher have no control over and assume no liability for the material available on those Internet sites or on other Web sites they may link to. Any comments or suggestions can be sent by e-mail to comments@enslow.com or to the address on the back cover.

Illustration Credits: Clements Library, University of Michigan, p. 66; Detroit Public Library, pp. 37, 42; Enslow Publishers, Inc., pp. 34, 110; Hemera Technologies, Inc., 1997–2000, p.6; Indiana Historical Society, p. 68; Karen Warrick Clemens, p. 45, 116; Library of Congress, pp. 17, 19, 24, 31, 33, 49, 55, 71, 81, 88, 89, 91, 92, 96, 105, 113, 117; National Archives, pp. 53, 106; New York Historical Society, p. 27; United States Naval Academy, p. 13.

Cover Illustration: United States Senate Collection.

Contents

Foreword

On September 13, 1814, Francis Scott Key was sent aboard the British fleet stationed in Chesapeake Bay to negotiate the release of Dr. William Beanes, an American official who had been captured after the burning of Washington, D.C. The release was approved, but Key was detained on the ship overnight while the British attacked Fort McHenry, one of the American forts defending Baltimore. In the morning, Key was delighted to gaze upon the American flag still waving proudly in the air above the fort. He began a poem to commemorate the occasion, which was first published under the title *Defense of Fort M'Henry*. The poem soon attained wide popularity and was sung to the tune "To Anacreon in Heaven." In 1931, this song, now known as "The Star-Spangled Banner," was officially made the National Anthem by Congress.

The Star-Spangled Banner

O say, can you see, by the dawn's early light,
What so proudly we hail'd at the twilight's last gleaming?
Whose broad stripes and bright stars, thro' the perilous fight,
O'er the ramparts we watch'd, were so gallantly streaming?
And the rockets' red glare, the bombs bursting in air,
Gave proof thro' the night that our flag was still there.
O say, does that star-spangled banner yet wave
O'er the land of the free and the home of the brave?

On the shore dimly seen thro' the mists of the deep,
Where the foe's haughty host in dread silence reposes,
What is that which the breeze, o'er the towering steep,
As it fitfully blows, half conceals, half discloses?
Now it catches the gleam of the morning's first beam,
In full glory reflected, now shines on the stream:
'Tis the star-spangled banner: O, long may it wave
O'er the land of the free and the home of the brave!

And where is that band who so vauntingly swore
That the havoc of war and the battle's confusion,
A home and a country should leave us no more?
Their blood has wash'd out their foul footsteps' pollution.
No refuge could save the hireling and slave
From the terror of flight or the gloom of the grave:
And the star-spangled banner in triumph doth wave
O'er the land of the free and the home of the brave.

O thus be it ever when free-men shall stand
Between their lov'd home and the war's desolation;
Blest with vict'ry and peace, may the heav'n-rescued land
Praise the Pow'r that hath made and preserv'd us a nation!
Then conquer we must, when our cause it is just,
And this be our motto: "In God is our trust!"
And the star-spangled banner in triumph shall wave
O'er the land of the free and the home of the brave!

—Francis Scott Key, 1814

Gentlemen, the British are below the city! We must fight them tonight.

—General Andrew Jackson in a speech to his troops before the Battle of New Orleans

1 "Old Hickory" and the Battle of New Orleans

 On November 26, 1814, a British fleet sailed from Jamaica, an island in the Caribbean Sea, en route to the American port of New Orleans near the mouth of the Mississippi River. Major General Sir Edward Pakenham, a well-respected English hero and soldier, was in command. He was aided by three other major generals: John Keane, Sir Samuel Gibbs, and John Lambert. Aboard the sixty vessels were fourteen thousand soldiers and hundreds of government officials—tax collectors, printers, and secretaries. They would be needed to set up a new colony for Great Britain along the Mississippi River. Army officers even brought their wives. Nobody aboard doubted that the ladies would need their silk gowns for the victory ball in New Orleans.

However, the British had a surprise waiting for them—Major General Andrew Jackson, whose toughness had earned him the nickname "Old Hickory." Even before the British had set sail, Jackson left Mobile, Alabama, another possible target of the British fleet. The general covered some three hundred fifty miles in eleven days "to have a view at the points at which the enemy might make a landing."[1] When he arrived in New Orleans on December 1, the general's clothing "was . . . nearly threadbare. A small leather cap protected his head, and a short blue Spanish cloak his body, whilst his high dragoon boots were long innocent of polish . . . his complexion was shallow and unhealthy; his hair iron grey, and his body thin and emaciated."[2] However, his appearance did not detract from the fierce expression of his "bright and hawk-like" eyes.[3] Since the citizens of New Orleans had done little to prepare against invasion, they welcomed Jackson warmly—even in the pouring rain.

A Man of Action

With confidence and energy, Jackson quickly took charge. He studied the few existing maps and then spent two days inspecting the surrounding area on horseback. He soon realized that the small forces available to him could not cover all the approaches to New Orleans. Jackson decided to block as many routes as possible. All available free men and slaves were put to work felling trees across the bayous, the many small waterways leading into or near the city.

Jackson also strengthened Fort Saint Phillip, which guarded the Mississippi River south of the city. He added a thirty-two-pound cannon (a cannon that fired thirty-two-pound cannonballs) and ordered the construction of two batteries, fortifications equipped with heavy guns, on opposite banks of the river to provide a crossfire.

Since Jackson was critically short of manpower, his next step was to recruit troops from the local population. He drafted a collection that included Creoles, people of French ancestry born in Louisiana; Frenchmen who had served in the army of Emperor Napoleon Bonaparte of France; Choctaw Indians led by Chief Push-Ma-Ta-Ha; free blacks from Santo Domingo in the West Indies; and the infamous pirates, the Lafitte brothers. When an army paymaster held back the wages of nonwhite soldiers, Jackson reprimanded him curtly, saying that wages were to be paid promptly "without inquiring whether the troops are white, black, or tea."[4]

Jackson's final defensive move was to send five gunboats under the command of Captain Thomas Catesby Jones to patrol Lake Borgne. This large shallow bay southwest of New Orleans stretched from the Gulf of Mexico almost to the Mississippi River.

The British Fleet Sighted

On December 13, 1814, Captain Jones spotted the British fleet as it dropped anchor in the Gulf of Mexico near Lake Borgne. He immediately sent word to his commander, who relayed the information to Jackson. Then Jones stationed his flotilla (a group of small, armed boats) at the mouth of the lake to see what the British would do next. He did not have to wait long. The very next day, a line of enemy barges advanced toward the five gunboats crewed by 185 Americans. Outnumbered and outgunned, Jones decided to retreat. Unfortunately, the wind and tide were against him and the flotilla became grounded in a foot or more of mud. Jones's choices were to blow up his boats to keep them from being captured by the British, or to make a last stand. He decided to fight. When the skirmish was over, ten Americans had been killed, thirty-five wounded, and the others taken prisoner. Not one man had escaped to warn Jackson that the British now had a clear route into New Orleans.

Capturing the gunboats allowed the British to advance across the lake unopposed, but it was not a simple task. Lake Borgne was too shallow for the fleet's large ships. The British were forced to row two thousand men sixty miles across the lake. It took three trips to transport the men. Several more trips were required for equipment and supplies needed by the soldiers.

The British Advance

On December 23, Colonel William Thornton, in command of sixteen hundred British soldiers, landed on the western shore of the lake and rowed up Bayou Bienvenue, which means "welcome." (Apparently, Jackson's orders had been disobeyed—the waterway was not blocked.) Thornton captured the American troops stationed on a plantation owned by Jacques Villeré only eight miles outside New Orleans. Villeré's son, Gabriel,

Outnumbered and outgunned, American Captain Thomas Catesby
Jones and his flotilla of gunboats made a courageous stand on Lake
Borgne near New Orleans in December of 1814.

held captive in his own home, jumped from a window when his guards grew careless, and raced toward New Orleans to warn Jackson.

Fortunately for the Americans, while the British had been rowing troops across the lake, more than four thousand reinforcements, backwoodsmen from Tennessee and Kentucky, had arrived in New Orleans. These men dressed in homespun clothes and coonskin hats were armed with long rifles, weapons more accurate at long range than the traditional muskets carried by the British soldiers.

After being warned by the panting, mud-stained Villeré, Jackson made the decision to attack the British that night.[5] One hour later, Old Hickory set out with eighteen hundred men. The rest of the army would follow the next day. The fourteen-gun schooner *Carolina* and the twenty-two-gun *Louisiana* glided down the Mississippi to support the infantry. It was already dark when the Americans reached the edge of the Villeré plantation. No one made a sound as the troops took their positions.

Certain that it was too late for the Americans to organize an attack, the exhausted British troops were bedding down for the night. They were completely surprised when the *Carolina* opened fire. A British officer described the scene: "Flash, flash, flash, came from the river; the roar of cannon followed, and the light of her own broadside displayed to us an enemy's vessel at anchor near the opposite bank, and pouring a perfect shower of grape and round shot, into the camp."[6]

Jackson waited a full half-hour while the *Carolina* shelled the British camp, then ordered his foot soldiers to attack. Again the British were unpleasantly surprised. The battle continued until midnight when Jackson signaled his men to pull back. By that time, the British had suffered 275 casualties and the Americans 215. Though indecisive, the skirmish left Old Hickory with one important advantage—the British never completely recovered from their shock and surprise. In fact, Jackson's daring attack convinced them that they faced an American force of fifteen thousand instead of only eighteen hundred. The British decided to wait for reinforcements.

The delay gave Jackson time to prepare. He pulled his troops back a few miles to a dry drainage ditch and began to construct a breastwork, a mound of mud and earth to block the British advance. The work went on through the night. As one group slept, others dug with picks, shovels, bayonets, and bare hands. Only the general stayed on duty all night. By sunrise, a mound of mud three quarters of a mile long stretched from a cypress swamp on the east to the Mississippi River on the west. The line was drawn.

Pakenham Prepares for Battle

British General Pakenham arrived on Christmas Day, 1814, with strong reinforcements, but did not press on toward New Orleans immediately. He decided to bring heavy guns from the fleet, to combat the deadly American cannon power. The cannons also had to be rowed sixty miles across the lake. During the next few days and nights, the British Navy transported twelve cannons across Lake Borgne. When the bayou narrowed, the guns had to be lifted and dragged through mud and reeds to the road leading to the Villeré plantation. One boat turned over on the lake and seventeen unfortunate soldiers carrying shot in their packs sank to the bottom and drowned.

By January 6, 1815, six thousand soldiers and a plentiful supply of ammunition had been transported across the lake. Pakenham was ready to launch his assault on New Orleans.

The Battle of New Orleans

On January 8, 1815, the Battle of New Orleans began about dawn when Colonel William Thornton ferried six hundred British regulars across the Mississippi. His goal was to seize artillery manned by a force of seven hundred ill-trained Americans on the west bank. Once the British soldiers controlled the guns, they could be turned on Jackson's main force across the river.

Pakenham had issued his attack orders the night before, but while he slept something went wrong. He had planned for Thornton's troops to cross the river while it was dark, but by five in the morning, the brigade had not left the east bank. It was dawn before Thornton seized the American guns, and he had no time to use them before Pakenham ordered a rocket fired, signaling the main assault.

Under the protection of fog, fifty-three hundred British regulars advanced across the Villeré plantation

Riding his white horse along the American battle line, General Andrew Jackson rallied his troops during the final stage of the Battle of New Orleans.

toward Jackson's main line, defended by forty-seven hundred men. Then the fog lifted. The British troops were completely exposed to American fire. All along the battle line the Redcoats (a nickname earned by the bright red uniform jackets the British wore) were mowed down before they could get near the American breastwork. Only one small column near the river got through to the American line, but they were quickly driven back by heavy gunfire. Many battle-hardened British soldiers turned and fled. According to one veteran of the European wars fought against Napoleon, it was "The most murderous [fire] I ever beheld before or since."[7]

Pakenham did his best to rally his men as he rode back and forth across the battlefield. One horse was shot out from under him, and shortly after mounting another he was "cut asunder by a cannonball."[8]

General John Lambert, who took command after Pakenham was killed, called for an immediate retreat. The battle had lasted only half an hour but one eye witness described the field as "a terrible sight to behold, with dead and wounded laying in heaps—all dressed in scarlet British uniforms."[9] More than two thousand British soldiers had been killed, wounded, or captured. The United States lost about seventy men.

Ironically, this battle should not have been fought. On December 24, 1814, in Ghent, Belgium, American and British diplomats had signed a treaty ending the War of 1812. However, the official documents, sent by ship, did not reach the American or British forces until weeks after the Battle of New Orleans.

British General Pakenham died during the Battle of New Orleans when he was struck by a cannonball.

Despite not actually affecting the outcome of the war, this final battle of the War of 1812 did give Americans a victory to celebrate and created a strong spirit of nationalism—a relatively new idea for the young United States. It also made Andrew Jackson a hero. In winning the Battle of New Orleans, Old Hickory had defeated one of the mightiest invasion forces ever assembled to that time.

Whensoever hostile aggressions . . . require a resort to war, we must meet our duty and convince the world that we are just friends and brave enemies.

—Excerpt from a letter by Thomas Jefferson to Andrew Jackson dated December 3, 1806

2 The Brink of War

The United States officially declared war on Great Britain for the first time in June 1812. However, a confrontation between the U.S.S. *Chesapeake* and the British man-of-war *Leopard* pushed America to the brink of war nearly five years earlier.

On June 22, 1807, the U.S.S. *Chesapeake* set sail from Norfolk, Virginia. Ten miles from port, in American-controlled waters, James Barron, commander of the American ship, watched as a British ship, the *Leopard*, approached. Barron thought he had nothing to fear when a British officer requested permission to board the *Chesapeake*. He allowed the officer to board. But the situation quickly changed. The British officer demanded to search the *Chesapeake*, claiming that four deserters from the Royal Navy might be on board. Barron knew he had deserters among his crew and wanted to protect them. He ordered the officer off the ship. A short time later, a cannon from the *Leopard* fired . . . and then another, and another. Barron was caught off guard. America was not at war with Great Britain, and he was not ready to fight a sea battle.

Twenty-one cannonballs tore into the *Chesapeake's* hull. Its masts were toppled and sails shredded. During the brief battle, three American sailors were killed and eighteen wounded, including Barron. The U.S.S. *Chesapeake* surrendered. After the British removed the four deserters, the American ship was allowed to limp back to port.

Although this incident caused many Americans to demand war, several years would pass before James Madison, as president, would officially ask Congress to declare war on Great Britain.

Mr. Madison's War

The War of 1812 has sometimes been called Mr. Madison's War. However, the events that led to this second conflict with Great Britain (the Revolutionary War was the first) began long before Madison's presidency. In fact, it was an indirect result of actions taken by Napoleon Bonaparte, emperor of France.

Napoleon, who was also one of the greatest generals of all time, was determined to build an empire by conquering Europe. By 1797, Spain, Austria, and Prussia (a country that included large parts of present-day Poland

and most of Germany) had been forced to sign peace agreements with France. Napoleon's armies had also occupied Holland. Only Great Britain, which had been at war with France since 1793, continued the fight—struggling to keep Napoleon from conquering its homeland.

Great Britain had survived because it was protected by the Royal Navy—which was stronger than the French fleet. The island kingdom would remain safe as long as Great Britain could control the seas. That meant keeping the ships well manned. However, this was not an easy task. Conditions aboard ships in the Royal Navy—poor food, hard work, and harsh discipline—caused British sailors to desert by the thousands. Many chose to work instead on American merchant ships, where the pay and working conditions were much better.

Some British seamen applied to be naturalized citizens of the United States. Many deserters wanted to be recognized as American citizens immediately, and bought "protection papers," fake documents (not issued by the United States government) that could be purchased for as little as one dollar. The British, however, refused to recognize these papers, or any form of naturalization, stating: "Once an Englishman always an Englishman."[1] The Royal Navy was authorized to "impress," which meant taking British deserters from American ships that were stopped on the high seas. Sometimes "mistakes" were made and American citizens were impressed instead. This issue, among others, would eventually force President James Madison to propose war.

Napoleon, one of the greatest generals of all time, was determined to build an empire for France by conquering Europe.

Neutral Trading Country

During the first several years of war against France, Great Britain did not interfere with American trade. Then, on May 16, 1806, Great Britain proclaimed a blockade of the European coast, stating that no nation could sell goods used for war to France, its colonies, or the countries under French control. Napoleon struck back with the Berlin Decree on November 21, 1806, blockading the British Isles. A series of British Orders in Council followed. One issued on November 11, 1807, declared that all vessels trading with places from which British ships were excluded were subject to capture unless they first put in at a British port and paid a fee.

On December 17, 1807, Napoleon proclaimed that any vessel submitting to a search by an English ship, or paying a fee to the British government, would be liable to seizure by the French Navy. Neutral commerce could not be pursued without violating one of these orders. The United States was caught in the middle. Between 1807 and 1812, the two warring countries seized about nine hundred American ships.

Great Britain controlled the seas. British warships waited outside every American seaport and stopped and searched ships. If French-made goods or goods bound for Europe were found, the ship and its cargo were sold at the British naval base in Halifax, Nova Scotia, Canada—a British colony at that time.

Though it had no military power to back any protest, the United States objected to the search and seizure of its ships. Great Britain and the United States also disagreed on the definition of blockade, on articles listed as contraband (illegal or unacceptable goods that could be seized), on what areas of a ship should be searched when it was stopped, and the impressment of sailors from American vessels.

President Thomas Jefferson

Though war fever had spread in America after the attack on the U.S.S. *Chesapeake*, Thomas Jefferson, the president in 1807, first tried to solve the problem through diplomatic channels. He wrote to James Monroe, his minister in London, England, and directed Monroe to demand not only the return of the seamen taken from the *Chesapeake*, but also "the entire abolition of impressment from vessels of the United States."[2]

When Great Britain refused, Jefferson decided to try economic pressure. He recommended that Congress pass the Embargo Act of 1807, halting United States trade with the whole world. This act made it illegal for an American vessel to sail to any foreign port and banned all European vessels from United States seaports. Jefferson believed that Great Britain's economy would be hurt if the United States, the largest consumer of British manufactured goods, refused to buy from it. The United States was also the world's largest neutral carrier. By refusing to transport goods to England, France, or their colonies, Jefferson hoped to cripple the British and French war efforts.

The embargo had little effect on the British. However, it did bring the American economy to a near

THE IMPRESSMENT OF AN

American Sailor Boy,

SUNG ON BOARD THE BRITISH PRISON SHIP CROWN PRINCE, THE FOURTH OF JULY, 1814
BY A NUMBER OF THE AMERICAN PRISONERS.

THE youthful sailor mounts the bark,
And bids each weeping friend adieu :
Fair blows the gale, the canvass swells :
Slow sinks the uplands from his view.

Three mornings, from his ocean bed,
Resplendent beams the God of day :
The fourth. high looming in the mist,
A war-ship's floating banners play.

Her yawl is launch'd ; light o'er the deep,
Too kind, she wafts a ruffian band :
Her blue track lengthens to the bark,
And soon on deck the miscreants stand.

Around they throw the baleful glance :
Suspense holds mute the anxious crew—
Who is their prey ? poor sailor boy !
The baleful glance is fix'd on you.

Nay, why that useless scrip unfold ?
They damn'd the " lying yankee scrawl,"
Torn from thine hand, it strews the wave—
They force thee trembling to the yawl.

Sick was thine heart as from the deck,
The hand of friendship wav'd farewell ;
Mad was thy brain, as far behind,
In the grey mist thy vessel fell.

One hope, yet, to thy bosom clung,
The captain mercy might impart ;

Vain was that hope, which bade thee look,
For mercy in a Pirate's heart.

What woes can man on man inflict,
When malice joins with uncheck'd power ;
Such woes, unpitied and unknown,
For many a month the sailor bore !

Oft gem'd his eye the bursting tear,
As mem'ry linger'd on past joy ;
As oft they flung the cruel jeer,
And damn'd the " chicken liver'd boy."

When sick at heart, with " hope defer'd."
Kind sleep his wasting form embrac'd,
Some ready minion ply'd the lash,
And the lov'd dream of freedom chas'd.

Fast to an end his miseries drew :
The deadly hectic flush'd his cheek :
On his pale brow the cold dew hung,
He sigh'd, and sunk upon the deck !

The sailor's woes drew forth no sigh ;
No hand would close the sailor's eye :
Remorseless, his pale corse they gave,
Unshrouded to the friendly wave.

And as he sunk beneath the tide,
A hellish shout arose ;
Exultingly the demons cried,
" So fare all Albion's Rebel Foes !"

This poster protested the impressment of American sailors on British ships. Impressment was one of the issues that eventually led the United States to declare war on Great Britain in 1812.

standstill, and almost put the country's merchant marine out of business. It also succeeded in turning regions across the country against one another. In the southern states and western territories, many citizens supported the embargo. They believed that Great Britain was treating them like unhappy colonists instead of citizens of an independent country. New Englanders, who depended on the shipping industry, nearly declared civil war because they were so angered by the embargo. Jefferson finally had to admit that the Embargo Act was a failure. In March 1809, after it had been in effect for fifteen months, Congress repealed the embargo. It was replaced in 1809 by the Non-Intercourse Act, which allowed Americans to trade with all nations except Great Britain and France.

Northwest Territory

Americans also took issue with the British on one other front. Before 1776, colonists homesteading in Indian Territory west of the Allegheny Mountains had been discouraged by England not to protect the lands of American's native tribes, but to make it easier for Great Britain to control the valuable fur trade.

After the United States became an independent country, even the threat of Indian attacks did not keep settlers from moving west and settling on the rich lands of the Northwest Territory (an area that eventually became the states of Ohio, Illinois, Indiana, Michigan, Wisconsin, and part of Minnesota). By 1810, American Indian raids were increasing on settlements in the

Northwest Territory. Most settlers believed the uprisings were "instigated and supported by the British in Canada."[3] In fact, Great Britain's defeat in the Revolutionary War did not end its friendship with American Indians. The British wanted to keep the profitable fur trade for themselves. The richest source of these furs was the Northwest Territory, and Great Britain continued to encourage the tribes to resist the stream of American settlers moving into the area.

Tensions had been mounting since 1805, when two Shawnee brothers—Tecumseh, a great orator, and Tenskwatawa, known as "The Prophet," a spiritual leader—began organizing an Indian confederacy. The Shawnee leaders established their camp at Prophet's Town along the Tippecanoe River in northwestern Indiana (seven miles north of present-day Lafayette). Tecumseh dreamed of an Indian confederacy stretching from Florida to Lake Erie—a confederacy strong enough to resist white settlers. He traveled great distances speaking to the tribes of the Kickapoo, Wea, Creek, Wyandot, Sauk, Fox, Potawatomi, Miami, Choctaw, Osage, and many others.

The settlers in the Indiana Territory became increasingly fearful of Tecumseh's power. They knew the Shawnee chief would drive them out when he felt strong enough, and asked for protection from the government before it was too late.

William Henry Harrison, governor of the Indiana Territory, was determined to crush Tecumseh's Indian confederacy. In November 1811, while Tecumseh was on a recruiting mission in the south, Harrison moved one thousand soldiers into position across the Tippecanoe River from Prophet's Town. The Prophet ignored Tecumseh's orders—to avoid war with Harrison at all cost—and prepared for battle, promising his two thousand warriors an easy victory. He told them that he had placed a spell on the white soldiers, making them too weak to defend themselves. The Prophet ordered his band to kill Harrison, the white leader who rode a gray horse.

On the morning of November 7, a sentry posted near Harrison's camp spotted Indians and opened fire. Normally, the warriors would have moved forward slowly, hiding behind trees and large rocks. However, The Prophet's vision had foretold an easy victory, so the Indians charged the camp. Harrison's troops easily drove them back three times. When the Indians discovered that The Prophet had deserted them, they panicked and fled. Later that day, Harrison ordered Prophet's Town burned to the ground. The Battle of Tippecanoe ended Tecumseh's dream of an Indian nation, but did little to stop the Indian uprisings on the frontier. The Shawnee chief, The Prophet, and hundreds of followers made their way to Fort Malden in Canada, where the British welcomed them. Tecumseh made camp there and waited for the big war that he knew was coming.

War Hawks in Congress

When President James Madison took office in 1809, he hoped for peace. The shipping centers of New England and New York resented the search and seizure of their

The War of 1812 has sometimes been called "Mr. Madison's War." However, the events that led to this conflict began long before Madison's presidency.

ships but preferred that to a war, which would destroy overseas trade altogether.

The south and west, however, continued to resent the way Great Britain was treating the United States. They believed that free trade, sailors' rights, and the chance to end the Indian uprisings forever were worth fighting for. Many of the newly elected representatives from these regions quickly earned the name "War Hawks." They believed the United States would have to fight to earn Great Britain's respect.

The War Hawks, led by Speaker of the House of Representatives Henry Clay, convinced Madison to demand that the British revoke the Orders in Council. This was the act that excluded neutral vessels, like those of the United States, from ports where British ships were banned. In March 1812, Madison sent a written demand to Great Britain on the U.S.S. *Hornet.* The ship returned on May 19 without a positive response from the British government. On May 22, Madison began composing his war message. On June 1, the message was submitted to Congress. In it, Madison outlined several American grievances: impressment of sailors, the search and seizure of American ships by British warships, blockades as defined by the Orders in Council, and the renewal of Indian warfare in the western territories.

On June 4, the House of Representatives passed the declaration of war by a vote of seventy-nine to forty-nine. On June 17, the Senate voted nineteen to thirteen in favor of war. Madison signed the declaration of war the next day—June 18, 1812.

The War Hawks, led by Speaker of the House of Representatives
Henry Clay (pictured), pressed Madison to declare war.

This map depicts the United States as it looked around the time of the War of 1812.

The War Nobody Wanted

The British, who had temporarily stopped Napoleon's advance in Europe, did not want war. British-Canadian settlers did their best to stay out of it, and most Americans had no desire to fight. However, the British had pushed the Americans too far. Through continued indifference to the young country's pride, Great Britain had repeated many of the errors that had led to the Revolutionary War. In that sense, the War of 1812 was a continuation of the American Revolution.

What Americans did not know, as they prepared for war, was that the Non-Intercourse Act had been working. By the early months of 1812, the economic effects of the embargo were being felt in Great Britain. British politicians realized that they needed American trade and called for the suspension of the Orders in Council.

The Orders were suspended on June 16, 1812, two days before the United States declared war, but the news arrived far too late. It had to be sent across the Atlantic on a sailing ship—a trip that routinely took four to six weeks. Had communication been speedier, war might have been avoided.

Come all ye bold Canadians, enlisted in the cause,
To defend your country, and to maintain your laws;
Being all united, this is the song we'll sing:
Success onto Great Britain and God save the King.

　　—excerpt from *The Bold Canadians*, a traditional song from 1812–1813

3 Disaster at Fort Detroit

Even before war was officially declared, Congress authorized President James Madison to call out the militia and appoint William Hull as commander of the Northwestern Army. In April 1812, General Hull, age sixty, arrived in Dayton, Ohio, to take command of two thousand troops. It had been decided that the British-Canadian forts and towns in the Great Lakes region would be the first targets in the event of war. Hull was to reinforce Fort Detroit in the Michigan Territory—a post located along the United States' northern boundary.

On June 1, the troops began the march north. In 1812, the trail that connected Dayton, in southwestern Ohio, to Detroit led through the Black Swamp.

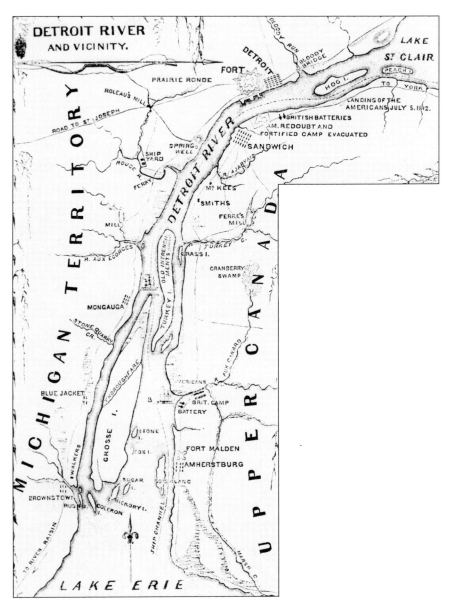

In 1812, America's Fort Detroit and Canada's Fort Malden sat on opposite banks of the Detroit River, only a few miles apart.

To transport artillery, supplies, and themselves over the area, Hull's troops had to build a road. They also had to keep constant watch for Tecumseh's spies who observed the army's slow advance.

By June 24, Hull's army had covered only half the distance, reaching Fort Findley in northwest Ohio. There, the general received a letter from Secretary of War William Eustis, dated June 18—the very day that war was declared. However, the message simply ordered Hull to advance as quickly as possible to Detroit and wait for further orders.

Hull and his troops hurried on, but the swampy trail continued to slow their progress. Then on July 1, the general found a small American ship, the *Cuyahoga*, moored along the Maumee River that flowed north to Lake Erie. He decided to ship his cannons and heavy equipment to Fort Detroit. Still unaware that the country was at war, Hull also loaded a trunk of his confidential military papers aboard.

Meanwhile, the dispatch to General Hull, informing him that the United States was at war, had been delayed. It had been misplaced in the Cleveland post office.[1] Finally, after several hours, the document was found in the Fort Detroit mailbag and a courier was dispatched immediately. He galloped through swamp and forest for more than three days and delivered the news to Hull on July 2 at two in the morning. After reading the dispatch, the general sent a boat to try to catch the *Cuyahoga*, but it was too late. Later that day, the British (who had learned four days earlier that war had been declared) captured the *Cuyahoga* and Hull's papers.

On July 5, Hull marched into Detroit, a settlement of about one hundred fifty houses on the outskirts of the log fort. He was prepared to cross the river into Canada and attack Fort Malden, which was manned by a small force—until he learned of the *Cuyahoga*'s capture.

Now that the British had captured vital information about his plans and the strength of his force, Hull lost his confidence and his best opportunity to take the British-held fort. He decided to fortify his position at Detroit, establish a dependable supply route, and forage for flour, blankets, whiskey, sheep, and cattle. However, the delay was fatal. It gave the British forces and their Indian allies time to mount an attack.

General Isaac Brock and Tecumseh

The British and Canadian troops stationed along the border were under the experienced command of General Isaac Brock. Once war was declared, Brock gathered troops that could be spared from York on the Canadian shore of Lake Ontario and hurried to reinforce Fort Malden in the settlement of Amherstburg (now Windsor). He was able to move quickly, since the British Royal Navy controlled the Great Lakes. His troops could travel by water instead of overland. On August 13, his force of 260 militia, citizens who had volunteered to fight, and forty regular troops reached Amherstburg and joined their Indian allies led by the "extraordinary character" Tecumseh. As the two leaders planned the assault on Fort Detroit, the Shawnee chief earned the British commander's respect. Brock reported that "a more sagacious [wise] or more gallant warrior does not exist."[2]

The Fall of Fort Detroit

On August 15, as Chief Tecumseh and his warriors surrounded the American fort, Brock sent a message to Hull demanding "the immediate surrender of Detroit."[3] When the American general refused, British warships began firing their cannons across the mile-wide river. Outside the fort, people ducked behind doors and scrambled for safety as cannonballs hit their homes. One man had just gotten up from bed when a shot came through the room and struck his pillow. Another cannonball smashed through the center of the table as a family sat around it, then dropped through the floor, and into the cellar. The bombardment continued until well after dark.

Inside Fort Detroit, the cannon fire seemed to have unnerved General Hull. His aide found him crouched on an old tent that was lying on the ground. The general was chewing tobacco furiously, adding more and more, sometimes removing a piece, rolling it between his fingers, then replacing it.

The American troops wanted to return fire, but Hull was too frightened and upset to organize a plan. Six men had died already, several more were wounded, and the shelling continued. On August 16, 1812, Hull surrendered without having fired a shot. "Not an officer was consulted," said one witness. "Even the women were indignant at so shameful a degradation of the American character."[4] The general was later court-martialed and found guilty of cowardice.

Under the terms of the surrender, General William Hull gave up Fort Detroit and its contents—all the ordnance (weapons and ammunition), the supplies, and its troops. The Americans stacked their arms and moved out. Then the British and Canadians entered the fort, pulled down the Stars and Stripes, and hoisted the British Union Jack in its place.

In addition to the loss of Fort Detroit, two other American posts fell to the British and their American Indian allies during the summer of 1812. Fort Michilimackinac on Mackinac Island was taken on July 17 after the British moved a cannon to a hill overlooking the fort during the night. Outnumbered at least ten to one, the Americans were forced to surrender.

After the loss of Fort Michilimackinac, Hull, as commander of the Northwestern Army, ordered the evacuation of Fort Dearborn, near Chicago, Illinois. Though a friendly chief warned Captain Nathan Heald not to leave the protection of the fort, the captain felt he must obey his orders. On the morning of August 15, about one hundred soldiers and civilians, including a wagon train of women and children, set out for Fort Wayne in Indiana. Only a few miles from Fort Dearborn, five hundred Potawatomie Indians attacked the group. Most of the party was killed. Twenty-nine soldiers, seven women, and six children were taken captive.

On August 16, 1812, American General William Hull surrendered to British General Isaac Brock without having fired a shot.

With the fall of these three forts, only Fort Wayne in the Indiana territory remained in American control. The whole northwest was now unprotected. Many settlers in outlying areas abandoned their homes for the relative safety of blockhouses, small log forts built in towns to provide a refuge during an attack.

War in Eastern Canada

While Brock's attention was focused on Fort Detroit, Stephen Van Rensselaer was appointed commander in chief of the New York militia, though he had no previous military experience. He moved troops into position near Fort Niagara in western New York State. Fort Niagara faced a Canadian post, Fort George, across the Niagara River that connected Lake Ontario to Lake Erie. By October 1812, six thousand American troops were stationed along the border near Fort Niagara, and Brock feared that the Americans would attack soon. He quickly moved most of his troops to Fort George.

Before daybreak on October 13, six hundred American troops landed in Canada near the village of Queenston and opened fire. Shots could be heard six miles downriver at Fort George, and Brock hurried to the battle scene. For a while, it looked as if the Americans would be victorious. By two o'clock, Van Rensselaer's troops controlled the strategic hill that overlooked the area. Then, Brock was mortally wounded as he led an assault to recapture the hillside, but not before he ordered General Roger Sheafe to march from Fort George with every available man.

With more British and Canadian troops on the way, Van Rensselaer called for reinforcements. However, for reasons unknown, the soldiers refused to cross the river. Without additional troops, the Americans were soon hopelessly outnumbered and another battle was lost.

In November 1812, American General Henry Dearborn, age sixty-one (and so feeble that his troops nicknamed him "Granny") led six to eight thousand troops north along the shores of Lake Champlain. His goal was to capture Montreal, a Canadian town on the St. Lawrence River. On the night of November 19, American troops seized a blockhouse held by a small Canadian force near Plattsburgh (now located in New York State). The enemy soldiers escaped. However, in the dark, the Americans became confused, fired on one another, then pulled back. Four days later, Dearborn and his army retreated. With that final fiasco, all plans to seize Canada in 1812 ended.

Unprepared for War

When war had been declared five months earlier, the freshman congressman John C. Calhoun declared that "in four weeks . . . time . . . the whole of Upper and a part of Lower Canada will be in our possession."[5] The United States government felt confident of a victory. The British, who had to defend a border some seventeen hundred miles long with fewer than eight thousand troops, were significantly outnumbered.

As with the events that led to the War of 1812, the reasons that the United States was so unprepared to

Many settlers in the Northwest Territory were forced to flee from their homes to the protection of the blockhouses, like this one, for fear of Indian and British invasion.

fight had begun much earlier. In the 1790s, the political group called the Federalists controlled Congress. This group believed that the best way to preserve American neutrality was to be prepared for war. By 1801, the Federalists had increased the army from 840 men to 5,400 and the navy to thirteen medium-sized warships called frigates, with six more under construction. They also began building a system of coastal forts to protect American cities from assault by sea.

In 1801, the opposing political party, the Republicans, took office. Republicans were determined to cut defense spending. Within a year, the army was trimmed to thirty-three hundred men, construction on ships was halted, and most of the frigates were decommissioned, or removed from service. The Republicans did spend money on coastal forts, but without a navy to act as a first line of defense, most seaport cities were an easy target for attack from the sea.

Disastrous Results

After declaring war in 1812, the United States was soon confronted by several problems caused by this lack of preparedness. The regular army was undermanned and had little training and even less battle experience. State militia, from which the government hoped to draw additional troops, would not get involved unless the state itself came under attack. The United States treasury did not have enough money to cover all its war expenses. The system of paying troops broke down from the beginning. As the war progressed, army pay was often six to twelve months late. The supply system was inefficient. Troops in the field frequently had to go for months at a time without shoes, clothing, blankets, or other vital supplies. The procedure for feeding the troops was even worse. The daily ration was supposed to consist of twenty ounces of beef or twelve ounces of pork; eighteen ounces of bread or flour; four ounces of rum, brandy, or whiskey; and small quantities of salt, vinegar, soap, and candles. The food the troops received was often spoiled and the portions smaller than promised.

However, the fundamental causes for the defeats

suffered by the United States were poor tactics and leadership of generals recruited because of their experience during the Revolutionary War. Now old and feeble, these leaders were recruited because younger officers lacked experience and were unable to control the men in their command.

By the end of 1812, the United States Army was in shambles. Thousands of American soldiers and settlers had died. The Northwest Territory was more dangerous and disorganized than ever. Most of the Michigan Territory was in British hands. In fact, the boundary of the American frontier had been pushed back to the Ohio River (a boundary the Indian tribes considered the border between white territories and their own lands). Many Indians, who had been reluctant to fight on either side, were now committed to the British. The British retained control of the Great Lakes, and the population of Canada, which had been drawn reluctantly into war, was now fired by enthusiasm over Brock's stunning victory.

After six months of fighting, the outcome of the war looked bleak, and Congress blamed Madison for not appointing better, more experienced, officers.

If you wish to avoid foreign collision, you had better abandon the ocean.

—Speaker of the House of Representatives Henry Clay in a speech given January 22, 1812

 "Don't Give Up the Ship"

In June 1812, the British fleet was the largest in the world with more than six hundred vessels. Challenging its warships for control of the Atlantic Ocean seemed like an impossible feat, so American leaders first planned to use the small United States Navy as floating batteries—sites for heavy guns— to defend American ports. They also hoped to capture or destroy some of the British cargo ships carrying supplies bound for Canada.

During the previous ten years, the Republican-controlled Congress had reduced the American fleet to sixteen ships. Seven were frigates. The *Constitution,* the *President,* and the *United States* were outfitted with forty-four cannons. The *Constellation,* the *Chesapeake,* and the

A frigate's sails would be raised and lowered in order to maneuver in battle situations. The U.S.S. *Constitution* is shown here.

Congress had thirty-eight big guns, and the *Essex* had thirty-two. The other nine ships were armed with fewer guns. The navy also had about two hundred small gunboats—no match for large British warships.

The frigates, built in the 1790s, were well constructed. Their officers and men were also well-trained sailors and skilled marksmen with cannons and small arms. Unlike the conditions in the army, food and other provisions were more than adequate. The navy's small size made it easier to supply, and once a frigate was outfitted, it could remain at sea for months. The pay for sailors was also better. Before the war, seamen earned ten to twelve dollars a month; skilled gunners earned eighteen. However, in 1812, to attract new recruits, the navy began offering incentives. If seamen signed on for two years, they received a bounty, or bonus, ranging from ten to thirty dollars and three months' advance salary. Monthly pay was also increased by 25 percent. Morale on board ships was high and sailors were prepared to follow their captains into battle.

First Encounter at Sea

During June 1812, Captain Isaac Hull, commander of the forty-four-gun *Constitution*, prepared to sail from Boston Harbor. Hull, an experienced seaman, had first gone to sea when he was fourteen. However, most of his crewmembers were new recruits. The captain trained and drilled the four hundred fifty men almost day and night. Then at noon on July 4, after firing a fifteen-gun salute in honor of the nation's birthday, he sailed. On the morning of July 18, the *Constitution* sighted four British frigates. Hull realized he was out-gunned and could not risk losing one of America's best warships. With no choice but to run, the captain decided to retreat fighting. He had part of the stern, or ship's back rail, cut away and mounted one of his biggest cannons facing the rear. Hull had two more cannons poked through the portholes in his rear cabin. Then, for two days, he did his best to outmaneuver the British. Finally, on the evening of the third day, a rain squall covered Hull as his ship pulled away and left the British behind. The *Constitution* reached Boston Harbor safely on July 26. The story spread quickly, and Captain Isaac Hull was praised.

Old Ironsides

Hull feared that the British fleet would soon blockade Boston Harbor. He worked his crew for twelve hours—without relief—to load supplies on board his ship. By August 2, the *Constitution* was at sea again. After sailing about seven hundred fifty miles from port, Hull's crew sighted the H.M.S. *Guerriere*, commanded by British Captain James R. Dacres. Immediately, both captains prepared for battle and tried to gain the advantage by positioning their ships. For forty-five minutes, Hull and Dacres sailed around each other, each trying to turn sideways and fire his cannons first, but neither could outmaneuver the other.

Finally, Dacres opened fire. His first shots fell short. He made a half-circle and fired again. This time his shots were too high, and Hull made his move. He raised more sail and closed quickly on the *Guerriere*. The American sailors on the *Constitution* held their fire until the ship pulled within fifty yards of the British vessel. Then Hull gave the order: "Now boys, pour it into them."[1]

Within fifteen minutes, the *Guerriere*'s mizzenmast, the mast nearest the stern of the British ship, toppled. The hull and sails were badly damaged. The British crew fought bravely, but after two more masts fell, Dacres surrendered.

During the battle, an American seaman saw a cannonball bounce off the *Constitution*'s side and exclaimed: "Huzza, her sides are made of iron."[2] From then on, the ship was nicknamed "Old Ironsides."

The crew worked through the night to remove prisoners from the *Guerriere* and tend the wounded. The badly damaged British ship was set on fire. Hull sailed back to Boston with his prisoners. His victory at sea encouraged Americans to believe they could win the war. It was much-needed encouragement. Only a few days later, news of General William Hull's surrender at Detroit reached the East Coast. (Isaac Hull was William's nephew.)

Success in the Atlantic

Isaac Hull's victory also brought an end to the plan to keep the American Navy close to its home ports. President Madison and his Cabinet members now realized that the nation's fleet could be effective at sea. By September 7, 1812, the ships were divided into three squadrons under the command of Captains John

Captain Isaac Hull, commander of the forty-four-gun U.S.S. *Constitution* captured the British H.M.S. *Guerriere* in a well-fought battle, August 1812.

Rodgers, Stephen Decatur, and David Porter. New orders were issued. The navy's primary role was to protect American merchant ships as they sailed the high seas. However, the captains were also instructed to pursue whatever course—in their best judgment—to annoy the enemy while protecting United States commerce. The skillful American captains set sail immediately to meet this challenge.

Captain Stephen Decatur, commander of the *United States,* preferred to sail solo and separated from the other ships in his squadron soon after leaving port. On October 25, about six hundred miles west of the Canary Islands, off the coast of Africa, Decatur and his crew encountered Captain John S. Carden and the recently overhauled British frigate, *Macedonian.* When the two ships sighted each other, the wind was blowing in favor of the British ship. By maintaining its course, the *Macedonian* could have closed quickly on the *United States,* nicknamed "The Wagon" since it was so difficult to sail. However, the British frigate had fewer cannons. Carden first made the mistake of keeping his distance, and then foolishly made a hasty approach.

Decatur responded in a cool, calculated manner. He outmaneuvered his foe, then fired so many cannons at the same time that the British crew thought the *United States* was on fire. By the time the *Macedonian* got within one hundred yards, its masts and sails were shot away. One third of its crew was dead or wounded. A British sailor described the damage done by the American guns: "the large shot came against the ship's side, shaking her to

Captain Stephen Decatur, commander of the *United States,* fired so many cannons at the same time that the H.M.S. *Macedonian's* masts and sails were shot away before it got within one hundred yards.

the very keel, and passing through her timbers and scat-tering terrific splinters, which did more appalling work than the shot itself."[3]

As Decatur positioned the *United States* to fire again, Carden surrendered. Decatur placed part of his crew aboard the *Macedonian*. They sailed for Newport Harbor in Rhode Island with the British prisoners on board. This was the first and only time a British frigate was brought into an American port as a prize of war.

Battle for the Pacific

In December 1812, Captain David Porter decided that he would annoy Great Britain by attacking its whaling vessels in the Pacific Ocean. When his ship, the *Essex*, rounded Cape Horn at the southernmost tip of South America in March 1813, it became the first American warship to sail the Pacific. The *Essex* hunted for several months. It seized fifteen ships and an estimated "two and one half million dollars worth" of sails, cables, anchors, provisions, medicines, and other stores.[4] This nearly destroyed England's whaling industry before ships from the Royal Navy could reach that corner of the ocean.

In February 1814, the British did finally corner Porter and the *Essex* at Valparaiso, Chile. For a month, the British blockaded the harbor. Then as Porter tried to make a run for open sea, a storm toppled his topmast. He was forced to drop anchor. He tried to reach neutral waters near shore, but the British moved in and attacked. The *Essex* was quickly destroyed. Three fifths of the crew were killed, wounded, or drowned. This defeat ended

American seapower in the Pacific and made it possible for the Royal Navy to target American fur posts on the Columbia River (the border between the present-day states of Oregon and Washington) and the American whaling industry in the South Seas.

"Cheapest and Best Navy"

The victories of the American Navy were significant, but even more important was the role of what one Republican called our "cheapest and best Navy"—American privateers.[5] As soon as war was declared, privately owned vessels of every description took to the high seas to prey on the British merchant marine. These privateers cruised the coast of Canada and islands in the Caribbean Sea, hoping to seize goods from British ships that could be sold at a huge profit. In the first six months of war, their captains and crews captured four hundred fifty ships. The *Yankee*, sailing out of Bristol, Rhode Island, seized eight British vessels valued at three hundred thousand dollars, and the *Rossie* out of Baltimore took eighteen enemy ships worth close to a million and a half dollars.

The Capture of the *Chesapeake*

One more important sea battle occurred outside Boston Harbor in June 1813. Captain James Lawrence, who had taken command of the *Chesapeake* on May 18, was ordered to put to sea "as soon as the weather and force and position of the enemy [would permit]."[6] Two British frigates were prowling at the mouth of the harbor.

On June 1, 1813, the *Chesapeake* sailed. Shortly after leaving the safety of Boston's harbor, Lawrence sighted the British frigate *Shannon,* and ordered his crew to prepare for battle. Lawrence gained the first advantage. He was positioned to cut across the *Shannon*'s stern and fire. However, for an unknown reason, he did not seize this opportunity. Instead, he moved in for a close-range duel. This made it possible for expert British gun crews to fire into the open American gunports. It took only three British broadsides to wipe out most of the *Chesapeake*'s crew and seriously wound its captain. As Lawrence was carried below, he gave the famous command that became the motto for the American Navy: "Don't give up the ship."[7]

After the British boarded the *Chesapeake,* the Americans continued to fight for a brief time, then surrendered. One hundred Americans were wounded and seventy were killed, including Captain Lawrence, in this fifteen-minute battle. The *Chesapeake* became the first American frigate to be captured by a British ship during the war.

Reaction at Home and Abroad

In 1812, the war at sea gave the United States' morale a much-needed boost, especially after the fall of Fort Detroit. The British were stunned by their defeats, even though the loss of a single ship, here and there, to the United States Navy did not significantly reduce the Royal Navy's strength. By 1813, Great Britain began to build heavy frigates equipped with more cannons, and its warships already at sea were ordered not to cruise alone or to engage in single combat with American ships.

British naval forces were also instructed to do something to bring the war to America. By May, American ports from Long Island to the Mississippi River were blockaded. Only along the New England coast were ships able to come and go at will. Many citizens in that part of the country made their living from the sea. They were calling for an immediate end to the hostilities. Great Britain hoped to encourage the New England citizens' demands. The British blockade also trapped the United States Navy in port and put an end to American victories at sea for the duration of the war.

We shall drive the British from our continent—they will no longer have an opportunity of intriguing [conspiring] *with our Indian neighbors, and setting on the ruthless savage to tomahawk our women and children.*

—Representative Felix Grundy of Kentucky, December 1811

5 In the Northwest Territory

General William Hull's surrender of Fort Detroit on August 16, 1812, quickly focused the objectives of the United States government. It needed to retake Detroit and end the threat of Indian attacks in the West. However, after William Hull's dismal failure, who could take command and lead an army to victory? President Madison considered appointing Secretary of State James Monroe as commander of the troops along the Canadian border, but settlers in Kentucky had someone else in mind— William Henry Harrison. They believed that Harrison's defeat of The Prophet and his warriors at the Battle of Tippecanoe in 1811 proved that he could lead troops to victory.

On August 25, 1812, the Kentucky legislature made Harrison a major general, though he was not a citizen of that state, and put him in charge of the fifty-five hundred volunteers in the Kentucky militia. Unlike many eastern states, where it had been difficult to raise an army, when the Kentucky governor called men to arms, more volunteered than were needed.

Harrison soon learned that British troops were marching toward Fort Wayne in the Indiana Territory, burning houses, destroying crops, and killing livestock along the way. Three hundred Indians reportedly had surrounded the fort. Harrison and the Kentucky militia marched north immediately. With only eighty men, the commander of Fort Wayne, James Rhea, could not hold out for long.

When the troops reached Dayton, Ohio, Harrison received a letter from Secretary of War John Armstrong telling him that he had been appointed a brigadier general in the United States Army. However, if Harrison accepted this appointment, he would serve under Brigadier General James Winchester, who had been commissioned six months earlier. The sixty-one-year-old Winchester had earned a reputation fighting Indians in Tennessee, but he was not as popular in the West as Harrison. Like William Hull, Winchester appeared older than his years and unsure of himself. Plump and graying, he had to have help mounting and dismounting his horse. In contrast, thirty-nine-year-old Harrison was vigorous, decisive, and totally confident. In a return letter to Washington, D.C., Harrison suggested that the backwoodsmen "would never perform anything brilliant under a stranger," meaning Winchester.[1]

Not waiting for further word, Harrison and three thousand men pressed on to Fort Wayne. By September 12, his force had warded off the enemy without firing a shot. Five days later, President Madison appointed Harrison commander in chief of the Northwestern Army—a force expected to grow to ten thousand with all the regulars and volunteers from Kentucky, Ohio, Indiana, Pennsylvania, and Virginia. Winchester would now serve under Harrison's command.

Plans and Problems

The commander's first order of business was to defend the frontiers and retake Detroit. To control Great Britain's Indian allies, he sent mounted troops to burn their villages and destroy their fields of corn, beans, and pumpkins, denying them food and shelter. The Potawatomi and Miami Indians escaped to Canada and joined the British.

To retake Detroit, Harrison divided his army into three forces. General Simon Perkins marched his brigade toward Sandusky, Ohio, on the west end of Lake Erie. Units from Pennsylvania and Virginia were to join him there. Perkins was instructed to build three blockhouses near Sandusky and construct a fifteen-mile road across the Black Swamp to the Maumee rapids. A second group of twelve hundred soldiers, under the command of Brigadier General Edward Tupper, was to follow the road Hull had built, stockpiling provisions in blockhouses along the way. The final force, under the command of General Winchester, was to approach the Maumee rapids from Fort Defiance (near present-day Defiance, Ohio). The three columns were to meet at the rapids, then march on to Detroit.

However, Harrison soon faced problems similar to the ones that had plagued Hull. The autumn rains made it impossible to transport the heavy guns, ammunition, and rations for an army of ten thousand across the swampy route. He was forced to make camp well south of the Maumee rapids. Troops under Perkins's command did get cannons to Upper Sandusky by December 10, but at an enormous cost. Many supply wagons were abandoned. Teams of horses, exhausted from pulling through deep mud, had to be destroyed.

Harrison was finally forced to wait for the winter freeze, when the army could transport baggage and artillery across the frozen rivers and along lake shores. While they waited, Harrison's troops were often without enough food, proper winter clothing, and medical supplies. The British controlled the easiest supply route through the Great Lakes. All supplies for the American Army had to be transported overland. Private contractors hired to handle supplies frequently delivered inadequate quantities, and what little was received was often spoiled.

In addition, there was still no adequate way to fund the war effort. New taxes were unpopular and Congress postponed passing a bill to raise money. Even Henry Clay and the other War Hawks had agreed to the delay. They wanted to get on with the fighting.

Some positive changes had been made, though. Secretary of War Armstrong had advanced talented young officers to positions of leadership. The troops were better trained. Bounties and increased pay had attracted more volunteers. By the spring of 1813, there were about thirty thousand men in uniform—more than twice the number at the beginning of the war—though most still were inexperienced.

"Remember the Raisin"

Though all the forces of the Northwestern Army had inadequate supplies, the twelve hundred Kentucky troops under Winchester suffered the greatest hardships that autumn. They slept in crude huts and survived on half rations—when they had food at all. Surprisingly, few quit.

Finally, on December 20, 1812, Harrison ordered Winchester to march toward the Maumee rapids. En route, Winchester received word that American settlers in Frenchtown along the Raisin River (near present-day Monroe, Michigan) needed to be rescued. Reportedly, a considerable quantity of food was stored there. In desperate need of supplies and bored by months of waiting, the troops voted to send a small force.

On January 18, 1813, Colonels John Allen and William Lewis, with 660 men, crossed the frozen Raisin River and surprised the enemy pickets. The British and Indians fell back, fighting every foot of the way, but by evening, the American troops controlled Frenchtown. General Winchester arrived two days later with three hundred additional troops and settled in, enjoying the comforts the frontier village offered. The next day, his scouts warned that British troops from Fort Malden were headed for their camp. However, Winchester did not believe the report was accurate and ignored it.

On January 22, an American sentry fired three shots in quick succession, sounding the alarm. They were under attack. Troops led by British General Henry Procter, commander at Fort Malden, immediately opened fire with artillery. Then, twelve hundred British regulars and Indians charged. The Americans retreated in confusion, and Winchester was forced to surrender.

Colonel Procter marched back to Fort Malden that same day, taking prisoners who could walk. Arrangements were made to transport wounded Americans to the fort early the next morning. Procter left them under guard. However, soon after the British left, a number of Indians, painted black and red and drunk on captured whiskey, came into town. They set the houses where the prisoners were being held on fire. Most of the wounded burned to death. Some tried to crawl out windows but were toma- hawked, scalped, then pushed back inside. The treatment of these wounded soldiers was not forgotten. "Remember the Raisin" was a cry used to rally the troops to battle during the rest of Harrison's campaign.

Action at Fort Meigs

Harrison was informed of Winchester's defeat when he reached the rapids on January 22, 1813. Without men to replace those lost at the Raisin River, and with the six- month enlistment of many of his militia drawing to a

After the British left wounded American prisoners at Frenchtown, Indians set fire to the houses where the prisoners were being held.

close, Harrison had to call off his winter campaign. Instead, he decided to establish a strong defensive position along the Maumee. He chose a site just below the rapids on the south bank and began building a well-planned fortification. Fort Meigs was exceptionally strong. It was ringed by picket logs, reinforced by mounds of dirt, and protected by blockhouses and batteries that overlooked all approaches.

Meanwhile, prodded by Tecumseh and his followers, Procter assembled an army of nine hundred soldiers and twelve hundred Indians. He knew Harrison was short-handed and wanted to attack Fort Meigs before American reinforcements could arrive from Kentucky.

On April 28, 1813, one of Harrison's scouting parties reported that between fifteen hundred and two thousand enemy troops were camped within striking distance. Tecumseh's Indians had already crossed the river and surrounded Fort Meigs. Harrison was outnumbered more than two to one. His only hope was the fifteen hundred reinforcements from Kentucky, but would they arrive in time?

For three days, Procter bombarded the fort with artillery, firing round after round. He hoped to force Harrison to surrender, but most of the cannonballs fell harmlessly on the dirt mounds surrounding the stockade. Then Harrison received news that reinforcements were only two hours away. He sent orders to them instructing part of the troops to row across the Maumee River, capture the British cannons, drive spikes in the touchholes (where cannons were lighted), destroy the gun carriages, then retreat immediately to their boats. Unfortunately, his orders to retreat were not delivered.

The reinforcements crossed the river. However, they confronted a band of Indians before reaching their target. After a brief fight, the warriors fled. The Kentuckians then attacked the British battery, driving the gunners off quickly. As they celebrated the easy victory, more Indians appeared at the edge of the woods, then retreated. Still unaware that Harrison wanted them to row back across the river, the soldiers followed the warriors—and walked into a trap. The British regulars attacked from the front while the Indians closed in behind them. When the skirmish was over, the Indians began to massacre the prisoners. This time, however, Tecumseh restrained his warriors. Observing Procter's indifference to the needless bloodshed, the Shawnee chief reportedly said: "Begone, you are not fit to command, go and put on petticoats."[2]

Twelve hundred of the reinforcements from Kentucky did reach Fort Meigs safely. Realizing that he had lost his best opportunity, Procter abandoned the fight and marched back to Canada on May 4, 1813. During the battle for Fort Meigs, 320 American soldiers were killed or wounded and 600 captured. The British

When the skirmish at Fort Meigs was over, the Indians began to massacre American prisoners until Tecumseh finally restrained his warriors.

lost only about one hundred men, not including their Indian allies. However, the British had not captured the fort, primarily because it was built so well.

Procter tried to take Fort Meigs once more, unsuccessfully, then targeted Fort Stephenson on the Sandusky River. After bombarding the stronghold from gunboats, Procter ordered the regulars to attack. As they marched forward, the British were mowed down by the sharpshooters and "Old Betsy," the fort's one piece of artillery. According to Procter's own account, "the fort, from which the severest fire I ever saw was maintained . . . was well-defended."[3] The 160 Americans led by twenty-three-year-old Major George Croghan held their ground. By August 1813, William Henry Harrison and the Northwestern Army had regained an American finger-hold along the border.

The Battle of the Thames

The attempts to take Fort Meigs and Fort Stephenson ended Procter's invasion into United States territory, but Procter and his Indian ally, Tecumseh, were destined to meet Harrison once more. In late September 1813, the Northwestern Army marched toward Detroit, only to discover that the British had abandoned the fort and were retreating east along the shores of Lake St. Clair.

Harrison and three thousand American troops pursued Procter and Tecumseh across the border. As they advanced, they found baggage and supplies discarded by the British, and captured two gunboats carrying Procter's spare ammunition.

Harrison caught up with the British on October 5, 1813, at the Thames River, about forty miles east of Detroit. Though badly outnumbered, Procter prepared to fight, arranging his thirteen hundred soldiers and Tecumseh's one thousand warriors in two thin lines between the Thames River and a swamp.

The cavalry, led by Colonel (and Congressman) Richard M. Johnson, asked Harrison for permission to charge the British line. Although this was an unusual plan, Harrison agreed. "The American backwoodsmen ride better in the woods than any other people," he said. "I was persuaded too that the enemy would be quite unprepared for the shock and that they could not resist it."[4]

Shouting "Remember the Raisin!" Johnson's troops galloped toward the enemy. They burst through the enemy line easily, dismounted, caught the British in a crossfire, and forced them to surrender.

However, the Indians continued to fight even against overwhelming odds, urged on by Tecumseh's battle cry. Then, suddenly, something was missing. The troops quickly realized that the voice of the Shawnee chief—whom they hated and feared, yet also admired—had fallen silent. Tecumseh was dead. The Indians withdrew. Exactly fifty minutes after Harrison had ordered the first charge, the battle was over.

Years later, Johnson claimed to have killed Tecumseh. Whether he did or not is uncertain. Sometimes it is claimed that the American soldiers took clothing, hair, and even patches of skin from Tecumseh's body for souvenirs, but the body of the chief was never found by

William Henry Harrison's victory for the United States at the Battle of the Thames helped overthrow British power in the Northwest Territories and destroy Tecumseh's Indian confederacy.

the white men. His followers spirited him away and buried him in a secret grave.

The Battle of the Thames was a great victory for the United States. Casualties were light and six hundred British soldiers were captured. This victory crushed British power in the Northwest and shattered Tecumseh's Indian confederacy—ending the unity of the Indians who had supported the British.

Give me men, sir, and I will gain both for you and myself honor and glory on this lake, or perish in the attempt.

—Captain Oliver Perry requesting additional sailors from his commander on Lake Erie, 1813

6 Battle for the Great Lakes

The disastrous results of General William Hull's surrender of Fort Detroit made it clear that the United States needed to gain control of lakes Erie and Ontario. The British had used the lakes to move troops quickly from one place to another and to ferry weapons, supplies, and food for the soldiers and their Indian allies from the Atlantic coast. There was simply no way to support large armies in the region without mastery of the lakes.

At the end of the summer of 1812, the balance of power still favored the Royal Navy. Great Britain had six vessels on Lake Ontario, carrying from eight to twenty-two guns. The United States had only the nineteen-gun *Oneida*. On Lake Erie, the British had six ships armed with two to seven guns. When Hull surrendered, the United States Navy had lost its one and only frigate on that lake. Five other vessels were bottled up at the eastern end of the lake, under the guns of British-held Fort Erie.

Building a Great Lakes Fleet

In September 1812, President Madison and his Cabinet ordered the construction of a Great Lakes fleet and appointed Captain Isaac Chauncey commander in chief. His orders were to "use every exertion to obtain control of them [lakes Erie and Ontario] this fall."[1]

In October, work began on two fifty-foot gunboats at Presque Isle on the shores of Lake Erie (near present-day Erie, Pennsylvania). Chauncey also ordered the construction of two brigs, large two-masted ships. He assigned a young naval officer, Commander Oliver Hazard Perry, to oversee the operation. On March 27, 1813, the twenty-eight-year-old commander arrived with his thirteen-year-old brother, Alexander, and one hundred fifty seamen. Perry immediately focused his attention on completing the work as quickly as possible—not an easy task. Several problems made it difficult to build "modern" fighting vessels hundreds of miles from civilization. Timber was the only ship-building resource found near Presque Isle. Everything else—canvas for sails, rope for rigging, and cannons—had to be hauled by keelboat and then oxcart over roads filled with mud holes and blocked by stumps and fallen trees. Because there were no sawmills nearby to make planking, all the timber work had to be done by hand.

When construction was completed, these four ships, along with five others stationed at Black Rock on the Niagara River, would give Perry's fleet an edge over the six British ships on Lake Erie. However, the Black Rock flotilla could not be moved to Presque Isle as long as the British occupied Fort Erie. The fort sat across the river from Black Rock. The American ships would be easy targets if they tried to leave the harbor.

Capture of York

While Perry was overseeing the building of the fleet, Chauncey took command of the naval forces at Sackets Harbor on Lake Ontario. His orders from Secretary of War John Armstrong were to attack the Canadian post of Kingston along the St. Lawrence River. York, near the west end of Lake Ontario, was the next target, then finally Forts George and Erie along the Niagara River.

Chauncey soon mistakenly reported that six thousand men guarded the Kingston garrison. Fearing that the four thousand men at Sackets Harbor would be insufficient to carry out the original plan, Chauncey and the commander of the army, General Henry Dearborn, convinced Armstrong that York should be the navy's first goal.

In April 1813, Chauncey sailed from Sackets Harbor with seventeen hundred troops under the command of General Zebulon Pike, a young officer who had already gained fame as an explorer. The American force landed west of York, the capital of Upper Canada, on April 27. Supported by Chauncey's fleet, Pike's force advanced with little opposition, seized the batteries guarding the harbor, and pushed on along the lake toward the garrison and the Canadian government buildings.

Within four hundred yards of the garrison, Pike halted and ordered his men to stand their ground until gunners could drag the heavy artillery into position through the mud. Knowing that victory was his, Pike sat down on a stump to wait until everything was ready for the final attack.

Then the ground shook. A gigantic roar filled the air as the garrison burst into flames. Chucks of masonry, broken beams, boulders, rocks, and stones of every size rained down on the American troops, killing or injuring more than one hundred men. The British officers, after deciding to evacuate the fort, had blown up the main magazine, the storehouse for all the ammunition. Pike was mortally wounded. As surgeons carried the general from the field, the British Union Jack was hauled down and the Stars and Stripes was raised. The Americans had won. But the price was high—320 Americans died, mostly due to the explosion of the garrison's magazine.

During the victory celebration that followed, the legislative building was set on fire—reportedly by American soldiers and sailors after they found a scalp (which may have only been a wig) hanging in one of York's government buildings. The same group was blamed for looting houses in the area, but without any hard evidence. Some historians suggest that the culprits were individual American sailors, not wearing military uniforms. However, the myth that the Americans burned the capital gained acceptance along the Canadian frontier as time passed, and created a strong feeling of hostility toward the United States.

The capture of York was an important victory for the United States. One British ship was destroyed and a large quantity of naval stores seized. This helped equalize British and American forces on Lake Ontario. It also hindered Royal Navy operations on Lake Erie, since the "ammunition and other stores for . . . Lake Erie were either destroyed or fell into enemy's hands when York was taken," one British officer reported.[2] Finally, the raid on York was the first in a series of campaigns that eventually allowed Perry to assemble his Great Lakes fleet.

The British Strike Back, Then Retreat

One month later, on May 29, British Commodore Sir James Yeo, with eight hundred regulars, attacked Sackets Harbor. Though most of the American troops were away aiding Dearborn's campaign along the Niagara front, those left to guard the well-fortified post defended their position well. The British force was driven back.

Although the attack failed, the raid was not totally unsuccessful. A young American naval officer burned a large quantity of his own supplies and nearly burned the *General Pike*, a new United States ship that was under construction. The officer had been told that the Americans were losing the battle.

Meanwhile, on May 27, 1813, an American force attacked Fort George on the shores of Lake Ontario and the Niagara River. Outnumbered and outgunned, the British troops abandoned this post and also evacuated nearby Fort Erie. After the Americans took the Niagara River, Perry was free to gather his flotilla. The ships from Black Rock sailed safely to Presque Isle, arriving just before the British fleet blockaded the harbor.

Launching the American Fleet

By July 10, 1813, the gunboats and brigs of the Presque Isle fleet were completed. After hearing about the "Don't give up the ship!" incident, Perry named one of his 480-ton brigs the *Lawrence.* The other brig was christened the *Niagara.*

Perry's next problem was how to get his large ships over a sandbar at the mouth of the harbor. It had protected the vessels while they were being built. Now, however, the guns had to be removed while the brigs were lifted over this obstacle. Unarmed, the ships could easily be destroyed by the British fleet that was lurking nearby, so Perry decided to wait. Then, for reasons that have never been explained, the British relaxed their blockade on August 1, 1813.

The very next day, the five smaller American vessels ringed the channel outside Presque Isle Bay, guarding the men who began lifting the two larger boats over the sandbar. Crews attached floats filled with water to the sides of the brigs beneath the waterline. As the water was pumped out and replaced by air, the floats rose, lifting the vessel. It took four days of strenuous labor to lift the *Lawrence* and the *Niagara* safely over the sandbar.

Now Perry faced only one other problem—he needed sailors. In a letter to Chauncey, he complained about this situation: "Conceive my feelings: an enemy within striking distance, my vessels ready, and not enough men to man them."[3]

On August 10, Perry's problem was partially solved when Jesse D. Elliott, a battle-tested commander, arrived with about one hundred experienced seamen and half a dozen officers. Though still short of men, Perry placed Elliott in command of the *Niagara*, and on August 12 sailed west to Sandusky Bay to meet with General Harrison. Harrison offered Perry a hundred Kentucky marksmen as crew, though most had never sailed anything larger than a flatboat or raft. However, after Perry explained what to do, the new recruits turned out to be pretty good sailors. With his fleet fully manned, Perry was now ready to meet the enemy.

Battle for Lake Erie

As the strength of the American Navy grew on lakes Ontario and Erie that summer, the Royal Navy could no longer depend on supplies arriving by that route. By September, the British at Fort Malden needed food—for themselves and their fourteen hundred Indian allies. On September 9, 1813, Captain Robert Barclay, with six ships, made a run to collect supplies from a post on Lake Ontario.

Perry, with his fleet of nine, sighted the Royal Navy ships the next day. Though Perry had more ships, the British still had the advantage because of their long-range guns. Even knowing this, Perry ordered his fleet to sail closer. As they approached the enemy, Perry ordered sand strewn on the decks to prevent the men from slipping on any blood that might spill. He had food served so that the crews would go into battle with full stomachs.

When the British opened fire with their long guns, the first three American vessels—two schooners and Perry's *Lawrence*—fought valiantly. The rest of the American fleet lagged behind. The *Caledonia* was a slow sailer, and Captain Elliott had kept the *Niagara* at a distance, using only his long-range guns. After two hours of fighting, the *Lawrence* suffered severe damage. All its guns were useless.

However, instead of surrendering, Perry hauled down his banner with Lawrence's famous words, "Don't give up the ship." He jumped into a small boat that had somehow survived the British bombardment, and with his brother and four seamen, rowed toward the *Niagara*. With shot falling all around him, Perry somehow reached the ship safely and took command. With an undamaged vessel at his command, he sailed back into battle. The *Niagara* broke through the British line. The crew fired the portside guns into the *Chippewa, Little Belt,* and *Lady Prevost.* The guns on the starboard side raked the other three British ships, the *Detroit, Queen Charlotte,* and *Hunter.* Then two of the larger British ships locked together while attempting to turn, and Barclay surrendered.

On the back of an old letter, Perry penciled his famous dispatch to General Harrison: "We have met the enemy and they are ours: two ships, two brigs, one schooner, and one sloop."[4] This battle ended Great Britain's control of Lake Erie.

With shots falling all around him, Captain Oliver Perry somehow rowed safely from his damaged ship to the *Niagara*.

A Hollow Victory

During 1813, Napoleon regained his throne as emperor of France and pursued plans to expand his empire. Great Britain was again forced to focus on the war in Europe and its strategy against the United States was to remain defensive. It could not afford to send more troops across the Atlantic, and simply expected the Canadians to hold their own.

The British failure to maintain control of the Great Lakes had the most serious consequences. The Royal Navy could no longer move men, supplies, and messages quickly and efficiently along the Canadian border. This set in motion events that led to Perry's victory on Lake Erie, the defeat of the British at the Battle of the Thames, and the collapse of the Indian confederacy.

Though the success of Perry and Harrison along the Canadian front in 1813 seemed promising, in reality, these wins simply restored the situation to the way it had been before the war. Also, American attacks on Canadian towns created feelings of hostility, and British and Canadian forces soon retaliated by raiding American border towns. The war's final battles were still to be fought.

Was it these ashes, now crushed underfoot, which once had the power to inflate pride? . . . Who would have thought that this mass, so magnificent, should in the space of a few hours be thus destroyed?

> —excerpt from a letter by resident Margaret Bayard Smith describing Washington D.C. after the capital was burned by British forces

7 The Country's Capital Captured

In 1814, Napoleon was finally defeated in Europe by the combined forces of Great Britain, Prussia, Russia, and Austria. This freed thousands of British troops for duty in the war against the United States. With these reinforcements, the English planned to punish their "rude American cousins."[1]

Great Britain's first target was the Chesapeake Bay area, the center for much of America's shipping and privateering. A large portion of the country's population lived along its coastline, or in the area's two largest cities—Washington, D.C., and Baltimore, Maryland. Only Commodore Joshua Barney and the five hundred men of the Chesapeake Bay flotilla, a group of small, armed boats, guarded the waterway that led directly to the nation's capital.

The Enemy at the Door

By June 1814, four thousand British regulars under the command of Major Robert Ross and twenty-four Royal Navy warships led by Sir Alexander Cochrane had established a base in Chesapeake Bay on Tangier Island, within easy striking distance of Washington.

Even with the British perched on their doorstep, President Madison and his Cabinet were slow to act. They did not believe that the British would attack the capital. Secretary of War John Armstrong declared: "They certainly will not come here. . . . No! No! Baltimore is the place. . . ."[2]

It was not until July 1 that President Madison began to take the British presence seriously and ordered an army assembled to protect the capital.

The British Advance

On August 18, the British fleet sailed into Chesapeake Bay. The Americans' only defense, Barney's gunboat flotilla, was completely outnumbered and forced to retreat. By the next day, four regiments of British regulars and a Royal Navy battalion had landed near Benedict, Maryland. The town was deserted. One regiment under the command of Rear Admiral George Cockburn set off immediately in pursuit of the American gunboats. When the British cornered Barney and his flotilla, the captain blew up his boats to keep them from falling into enemy hands.

Meanwhile, the main British force marched toward Washington. Their commander, Ross, a veteran of the

Napoleonic Wars, had some doubts about this venture. His troops were badly out of shape after the long trip across the ocean. He had no cavalry and only three small field guns. However, no one blocked the road or burned any bridges to slow the British advance. It was not until after Ross and his troops had marched fourteen miles to Bladensburg, Maryland, that they began to see any signs of American resistance.

Tardy Preparations

On August 22, 1814, when the British had advanced to within sixteen miles of Washington, Madison and his Cabinet finally realized the danger. News of the landing had reached Brigadier General William Winder, commander in chief in the Washington area, five days earlier. Since then, he had been frantically trying to raise an army to fight the British. Though Winder should have had fifteen thousand men under his command, only three thousand were actually available—since the government would not call on them until the danger was "imminent."

On August 24, Winder spent most of the predawn hours riding the countryside trying to devise a plan. When his horse gave out, he stumbled about on foot, fell into a ditch, and hurt his right arm and ankle. For a while, the general's own aides could not find him and feared that he had been captured by the British.[3] Winder gained little useful information during this misadventure. By morning, he was still uncertain of where the British planned to attack. He ordered Brigadier General Tobias

Stansbury, with two thousand militia, to occupy Bladensburg, Maryland. Brigadier General Walter Smith and fifteen hundred District of Columbia militia were to wait at the Potomac Bridge on the eastern outskirts of Washington, ready to march where needed. The only experienced troops available that August morning were a handful of regulars and four hundred naval men, the crew of the Chesapeake flotilla.

At ten o'clock, Winder's scouts finally brought him the information he needed. The British were advancing on Bladensburg. Winder immediately ordered Smith to march with his troops to reinforce Stansbury. An hour later, General Winder, the president, and most of the Cabinet followed.

Stansbury's untrained troops formed two lines on the hills above Bladensburg, overlooking the town bridge. Sharpshooters and cannons were on the front line, while other troops formed a second line some distance back. Another regiment also took position to the left of the front line—until Secretary of State James Monroe, who had always wanted to be commander in chief of the American forces, ordered it back a quarter of a mile. This new position was too far away to be useful, but by the time Winder arrived to inspect the lines, it was too late to make any changes. A mile to the rear, Smith's brigade formed a third line as the troops arrived from Washington.

President Madison, dressed in black with two borrowed dueling pistols at his waist, Attorney General Richard Rush, and the secretaries of state, war, and the treasury all gathered behind the lines. However, when a scout who had been sent to watch for signs of the British galloped back to announce the enemy's approach, he discovered the presidential party out in front of the American lines, riding toward Bladensburg. The scout warned President Madison and his Cabinet to retreat to safety.

Defeat and Retreat

Shortly after noon on August 24, the fighting began. The American cannons and sharpshooters fired relentlessly as the British troops marched across the bridge at Bladensburg. Many British soldiers were killed or wounded. However, as soon as one British soldier fell, another took his place in the battle line.

The British easily pushed the American sharpshooters back. Then General Ross began firing off rockets, and the inexperienced, untrained American militia that formed the two front lines panicked and fled. The rockets, long tubes filled with powder, worked like fireworks. They completely missed their marks, but made a terrifying sound.

The third American line, Washington's final defense, held out a bit longer before retreating. Only the naval veterans under Commodore Joshua Barney stood their ground until they were out of ammunition. Barney, badly wounded, made sure that most of his men escaped before he surrendered to the British.

Soon the road to Washington was filled with retreating Americans. Fortunately, the president and Cabinet had already galloped back toward the city.

The President's Wife

In Washington at three o'clock in the afternoon, First Lady Dolley Madison waited in the president's house for word from her husband, the president. She listened to the boom of the cannons and watched the rockets flash across the sky as she wrote a letter to her sister: "Will you believe it, we have had a battle near Bladensburg, and I am still here within sound of the cannon! Mr. Madison comes not. May God protect him! Two messengers, covered with dust, come to bid me fly; but I wait for him."[4]

As the messengers had galloped up to the president's house, one had shouted: "Clear out, clear out! General Armstrong has ordered a retreat!"[5]

Dolley Madison had earlier ordered her carriage loaded with trunks that contained the Cabinet's official papers. She watched calmly now as the silver, books, more papers, a small clock, and even the mansion's red velvet curtains were loaded into a wagon. She took time to add this to the letter to her sister: "Mr. Carroll has come to hasten my departure and is in a very bad

Although President James Madison was awa at the time, First Lady Dolley Madison was i Washington, D.C., when the British attacke nearby Bladensburg.

First Lady Dolley Madison was able to save this large portrait of George Washington by removing it from the White House before British forces burned Washington, D.C.

humour because I insist on waiting until the large picture of George Washington is secured, and it requires to be unscrewed from the wall."[6] They finally had to dismantle the frame to remove Washington's portrait. The First Lady of the United States climbed into her carriage only after she was sure the canvas was safe.

By now, the streets of the capital were crowded with soldiers, senators, women, and children in carriages, horses, wagons, and carts loaded with household goods, all trying to escape the British by fleeing across the wooden bridge on the west side of the city.

Up in Flames

On the evening of August 24, Ross and Cockburn, with two British regiments, marched into a deserted Washington, D.C. Unopposed by any American troops, the British set fire to the Capitol and the Treasury buildings. They helped themselves to an abandoned banquet at the Madisons—a victory dinner ordered by the president earlier that morning. Then, the British burned the president's house. The next day, public buildings and private homes valued at more than a million dollars were burned. The fires burned until torrential rains began to fall later that night. Gale-force winds blew roofs off already damaged houses. Several buildings toppled, burying British soldiers in the debris. Two cannons were lifted from their mounts and hurled several yards. Discouraged by the violent storm, Ross ordered his troops back to their ships on the evening of

Triumphant British soldiers watch Washington, D.C., burn in 1814.

August 25, 1814, leaving behind the charred remains of the capital of the United States.

Business Not Quite As Usual

Following the disastrous defeat, General Winder abandoned the capital and retreated as far as Montgomery Court House, twelve miles north of Washington. There, he tried unsuccessfully to collect his army. Meanwhile, President Madison, the First Lady, and the Cabinet members were wandering about the countryside for two days looking for each other.

On the evening of August 27, after receiving a note from Monroe stating that the British had left the capital

When President Madison rode back into Washington, D.C., he found his house a roofless burned shell.

and were returning to their ships, the president rode back into Washington. He found the president's house a roofless shell and saw that "the roof, that noble dome [on the House of Representatives], painted and carved with such beauty and skill, lay in ashes in the cellars beneath the smouldering ruins."[7] Even as he surveyed the damage, Madison heard more cannon fire followed by a dreadful explosion. The British had attacked and blown up Fort Washington, located on the Potomac River just outside the city.

The Madisons moved into a home that the British had not destroyed. The president and his Cabinet began reorganizing the government. Secretary of War Armstrong, who was blamed for this disaster, resigned. Monroe temporarily took over the War Department. On September 20, 1814, the third session of the Thirteenth Congress began its work in a crowded room in the Post Office Building. Its first task was to demonstrate that the government was once again in control of the nation's capital and that it would continue to function.

Fort McHenry and Baltimore

While the president and his Cabinet were preoccupied in Washington, the British lost no time launching an assault on Baltimore. Their plan was to strike from land and sea. On September 12, Sir Alexander Cochrane and the Royal Navy anchored fourteen miles outside the city. British General Ross and forty-five hundred men disembarked. While the general marched north, the fleet sailed on toward its target—Baltimore's Fort McHenry.

A few miles from the city, General John Stricker and a company of American riflemen surprised Ross. They began to snipe at the British from every direction. Stricker was soon forced to retreat, but not before one of his sharpshooters killed British General Ross. The British soon resumed their march toward Baltimore under the command of Colonel Arthur Brooke, but the brief battle had been costly. The British lost over three hundred men, including General Ross. American casualties numbered about two hundred. However, Stricker had quickly shown the British that Baltimore was not as unprepared for battle as Washington had been.

On September 13, 1814, the Royal Navy opened fire on Fort McHenry while Brooke began the assault against Baltimore on land. For a day and a night, the British fired mortars, rockets, and shells. The one thousand Americans inside the fort under the command of Major George Armistead did not fire in return. It would have been useless, since the enemy ships were beyond the range of the fort's guns. During the next twenty-five hours, the British fired more than fifteen hundred rounds at the fort. However, damage to the fort was minimal. Only four Americans were killed and twenty-four wounded. The Royal Navy also failed in its attempt to capture Baltimore's waterfront battery and to land troops south of the city.

On shore, British Colonel Brooke tried twice to break through the well-fortified American lines. Each time, his troops were pushed back. Brooke met with Cochrane on September 15, and the two commanders agreed that Baltimore was not worth the effort. The British pulled out later that day.

"The Star-Spangled Banner"

Francis Scott Key, a prominent Washington lawyer, had watched the siege of Fort McHenry throughout the September night. Key had come to the British fleet to arrange for the release of an American prisoner of war. After he completed his mission, the British refused to put him ashore until the attack on Fort McHenry was over. Key paced the ship all night, watching the bombardment. On the morning of September 14, he was overjoyed to see the American flag still flying, a flag so big it could easily be seen from a ship in the harbor.

This flag had been specially made by a Baltimore woman, Mary Young Pickersgill, and her thirteen-year-old daughter, Caroline. The fifteen stars measured two feet from point to point. Each red and white stripe was two feet wide.

Key, a poet, was inspired by the sight. He immediately jotted down the first draft of some verses on the back of a letter he had in his pocket. These were later revised, set to the tune of an old British drinking song, and entitled "The Star-Spangled Banner." The song eventually became the American national anthem.

The Final Conquest

The British now set their sights on New Orleans, where produce worth a million dollars sat on the docks. With blessings from Spain, a country allied with Great Britain in its fight to defeat Napoleon in Europe, the British fleet occupied Pensacola, Florida, and planned its attack.

On the morning of September 14, 1814, as he stood on the deck of
the British ship where he had been detained all night, Francis Scott
Key was proud and relieved to see the American flag still flying over
Fort McHenry.

There shall be a firm and universal peace between His Britannic Majesty and the United States, and between their respective countries, territories, cities, towns, and people, of every degree, without exception of places or persons. All hostilities, both by sea and land, shall cease . . .

—excerpt from the Treaty of Ghent, December 24, 1814

8 Winning the Peace Talks

 By 1814, while the British and United States exchanged fire in North America, another battle line was being drawn in Europe—down the center of the peace talk table in Ghent, Belgium.

Attempts to end the hostilities had begun almost as soon as the United States declared war on Great Britain. On June 23, 1812, President Madison invited Augustus J. Foster, the British minister on assignment in Washington, to the president's mansion and expressed his desire to avoid "any serious collision."[1] The president informed Foster that the British could restore peace at any time by giving up impressment and the Orders in Council. (Though the Orders in Council had been suspended on June 16, 1812, no official agreement had ever been signed by the two countries.)

The British government, preoccupied with the war with Napoleon, also hoped to avoid a confrontation with America. They believed the steps needed to stop the war had already been taken when the Orders in Council were suspended. The Royal Navy was instructed to ignore any attacks from privateers until the news could reach America. However, the impressment of sailors was an issue Americans refused to drop, and Foster was informed that the practice must end before negotiations could begin.

However, in November 1813, President Madison accepted Great Britain's offer to begin peace negotiations. He appointed John Quincy Adams, James Bayard, Henry Clay, Jonathan Russell, and Albert Gallatin, exceptionally strong-willed and opinionated men, to bargain on behalf of the United States. At first, these delegates were instructed to negotiate the terms of blockades, contraband, and maritime rights of neutral countries during war. They were also told that the treaty must put an end to impressments, and to try to secure the surrender of Canada to the United States. The five American delegates quickly realized that these were impossible goals.

Outcry for Revenge

Now that the war with Napoleon had ended, and Great Britain had won, the English were angry with the United States. They believed that the war in America had aided their enemy in Europe. *The London Sun* printed that the American people must not be "left in a condition to repeat their insults, injuries and wrongs."[2]

After agreeing to meet in Ghent, Belgium, Great Britain was in no hurry to sit down and talk. They hoped that victories in America would strengthen their bargaining position. When reports of the mood in Great Britain reached Washington in June 1814, Madison and his Cabinet decided to drop the issue of impressment. New instructions were sent to the American delegation but did not arrive in time for the first meeting.

The Talks Begin

It was August before Great Britain's commissioners, Lord James Gambier, a naval officer; Henry Goulburn, a government undersecretary; and Dr. William Adams, a lawyer, arrived in Ghent. All three were inexperienced negotiators who had the authority only to deliver messages between the American delegates and the British government.

At the first meeting on August 8, 1814, the British commissioners believed they had the upper hand and flatly refused to discuss the issue of impressment. Instead, they demanded that "retention of conquered territory" be a starting point for negotiations.[3] The Canadian border was to be adjusted in Canada's favor to include parts of the states of Maine and New York. American Indians, who had aided the British, were also to be given most of the lands in the old Northwest Territory. Great Britain claimed the right to navigate the Mississippi River, and Americans were to forfeit fishing rights on British shores in the North Atlantic.

These demands were completely unacceptable to the American delegation, and since the British refused to discuss impressment, it appeared that the peace talks' first session would be the last. However, that very evening, the new instructions arrived from Washington, authorizing the Americans to drop the issue of impressment.

Clay also suspected that Great Britain was trying to gain time, hoping that military victories in America would strengthen its bargaining power. He suggested that the American delegates draft a reply, then wait and see what the British commission's next move would be.

At the Table Again

Clay's theory proved right. The British government did not want the negotiations to end. Within a few days, the commissioners indicated that they were willing to give in on some issues. At a second meeting, on August 19, Gambier presented a "modified" British proposal. In this plan, the United States would give up the northernmost portion of Maine. Great Britain would control all military installations on the Great Lakes (to protect Canada from acts of war) and be guaranteed the right to navigate the Mississippi River.

Finally, the British demanded that the border of the Indian state fall along the line set by the Treaty of Greenville, an agreement signed in 1795 after General Anthony Wayne's victory at the Battle of Fallen Timbers. The tribes who had signed the treaty lived in the Northwest Territory. This meant that lands now part of the

Indiana, Illinois, Wisconsin, and Michigan territories and the state of Ohio would have to be returned.

The Americans were astounded.[4] When Gallatin asked what should be done with the hundred thousand white settlers who lived in the proposed Indian state, Dr. Adams replied that "They must shift for themselves."[5]

The American delegates asked that the British proposals be put in writing, then spent four days working on a reply on which they could all agree. Adams wrote the first draft, then he and the others spent hours revising. Finally, on August 25—the night the British burned Washington—the American delegates signed their response. The note was brief and to the point. It rejected the idea of an Indian state and of British military control over the Great Lakes.

As they sent their reply to the British, the Americans believed that this would end the negotiations. Only Clay still thought the British were bluffing. He was right again. The British realized that if the talks ended now, England would be blamed for ending the hope of peace. The government prepared new instructions for the British commissioners.

Playing the Game

On September 5, 1814, negotiations began again by correspondence. In the first letter Great Britain offered only insignificant changes. All the American delegates, except Clay, were pessimistic. Clay, a card player who knew the value of a poker face, believed that if the

Americans stood their ground, the British would back down. Though he had no real intention of leaving, Clay announced plans to return to the United States immediately, and his bluff worked.

Not wanting negotiations to end, the British government told their commissioners to give up the idea of an Indian state. This information was passed on to the American delegation on October 8. The British proposed that the Indians keep the same territories they held in 1811 before the outbreak of war. This item, the first that the two commissions agreed on, was a beginning.

Now each delegation began to prepare its version of a treaty. In the beginning, the Americans were at a disadvantage since the news of the burning of Washington had finally reached Ghent. However, this changed when details of Great Britain's unsuccessful campaign on Baltimore arrived.

The issue of impressment was ignored by both delegations, and the British government soon dropped its demand for military control of the Great Lakes. However, the peace negotiations dragged on as the British delegates raised issue after issue. Late in October, they questioned American rights to cure fish on certain British-owned shores, and to fish in certain waters. This made American delegate Adams angry. Next, the British again claimed the right to navigate the Mississippi River. This demand upset Clay. It took all of Gallatin's tact and patience to get these relatively insignificant issues shelved.

Political and Public Pressure

By the end of 1814, British treaty negotiations with France were not going smoothly. There was even fear that Napoleon would regain power, and that the fighting in Europe might begin again. Political pressure was directed at the British government to end the war with the United States. The country's citizens demanded relief from the heavy taxes needed to support war—first in Europe and now in America. They encouraged their government not to humiliate the United States at the peace table. Most regretted the destruction of Washington, fearing that that incident alone would encourage the Americans to continue the fight. For these reasons, word was sent to the British commissioners at Ghent to get as good a settlement as possible, but not to push for unreasonable demands.

Meanwhile, the United States also faced great difficulties. Trade was at a standstill. The government was out of funds. There were not enough new recruits to replace soldiers in the regular army who had been killed or wounded in battle. Finally, there was a growing movement in the New England states to secede from the rest of the union.

New instructions were also sent to the American delegates. They were free to negotiate a peace agreement based on a return to a prewar status. The sticky issues of boundaries and maritime rights of neutral nations could be left for future negotiations.

The Treaty of Ghent

On December 1, 1814, the two delegations met for the first time since August 19. The Americans now had a significant advantage over the British commissioners. They knew exactly what they wanted to accomplish—peace with no concessions.

During the next several meetings, the Americans became more and more confident. John Quincy Adams and his colleagues drafted a treaty based on the "status quo ante bellum," the status before the war. Nine of the fifteen articles in this draft were amended and accepted as part of the final document.

The Treaty of Ghent stipulated that all conquests of land were to be returned. Both sides were to end hostilities against the Indians. The British abandoned the idea of an Indian state. Nothing at all was said about fishing rights, navigation of the Mississippi River, or boundary problems. Nowhere in the treaty was any reference made to impressment or the maritime rights of neutral countries—the issues that had led to war.

The signing ceremony was set for December 24. After a few small errors were corrected with pen and ink, the Treaty of Ghent, also called the Peace of Christmas Eve, was signed. The documents, which simply restored the conditions that existed before the war, were now official and subject to ratification in Washington and London. As John Quincy Adams accepted his copies, he stated his hopes that this would be the last treaty of peace between Great Britain and the United States. Now the American delegates could return home. The war was officially over.

John Quincy Adams helped draft the peace treaty that ended the War of 1812.

On December 24, 1814, the Treaty of Ghent—also called the Peace of Christmas Eve—was signed.

The Treaty Sails for America

The British commissioners delivered the documents to their government on December 26, 1814, and the treaty was quickly signed.

Unfortunately, there was no speedy way to deliver the news to Washington or to the British fleet sailing for the American port of New Orleans. On January 2, 1815, as Henry Carroll, Clay's personal secretary, and Anthony Baker, a representative of the British government, sailed for America with a copy of the treaty, preparations for the final confrontation of the War of 1812 were under way. Delayed by bad weather, their ship did not dock in New York City until February 11. Official copies of the treaty arrived in Washington on February 14, ten days after news of General Andrew Jackson's victory at the Battle of New Orleans.

On February 16, the United States Senate voted unanimously to ratify the Treaty of Ghent, and President Madison signed the document later that day. The war officially came to an end at 11:00 P.M. on February 17, 1815, when Secretary of State James Monroe exchanged signed copies with Baker.

By the time this news reached England, Napoleon had reclaimed power in France, and the British government had learned of the disaster at New Orleans. Great Britain was relieved that the United States had ratified the treaty so quickly.[6]

The fear of our late enemy;
The respect of the world; and
The confidence we have acquired in ourselves.
—excerpt from a Vermont newspaper summarizing what the United
States gained from the war

9 Lasting Effects of the War of 1812

The War of 1812 is sometimes called America's second war of independence. In both conflicts, either as English colonists or as citizens of the United States, the population objected to being forced to obey Great Britain's dictates. However, in 1812, it was the country's national pride that was threatened rather than any real attempt on Great Britain's part to reclaim the United States as a colony.

A look back to 1812 shows clearly how unprepared the United States was to fight a war. The fact that the country did not lose its independence or at least a portion of its territory was miraculous. In the end, it was more luck than military expertise that prevented the map of the United States from being redrawn in Canada's favor.

The communication and transportation of the day influenced events that led to the War of 1812. In fact, conflict might have been avoided completely if sailing ships had not been the speediest way to deliver news across the Atlantic Ocean. However, this strange little war, the United States' second and last struggle against Great Britain, and the second and last time it tried to conquer Canada, was a turning point in American history.

A Military Draw

America's army and navy won few victories during the two years and eight months of the War of 1812 because the country was so unprepared. Beginning in 1801, the Republican-controlled Congress cut defense spending. The regular army was reduced to thirty-three hundred men. This small force had little training and even less battle experience. Construction on new navy ships was stopped, and most of the frigates were removed from service.

Leadership, civil and military, was also ineffective. The old and feeble military generals recruited during the War of 1812 were poor leaders and tactical planners. Younger officers lacked experience and were often unable to control the men under their command. Endless debates in Congress delayed or prevented the adoption of laws needed to raise an army and create taxes to pay for the war effort. James Madison, who was a weak, indecisive president, was unable to push necessary legislation through Congress. He was also slow to remove incompetent generals in the field and ineffective members of his

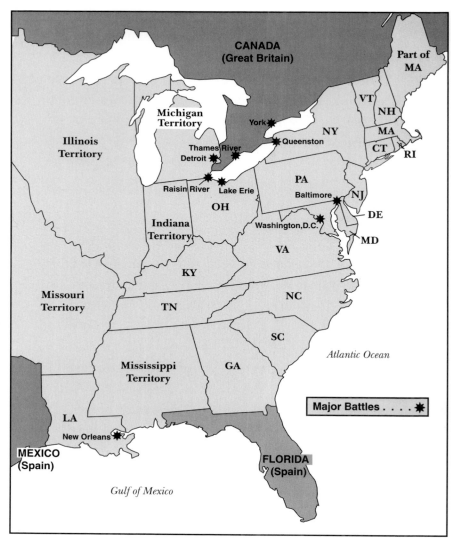

The War of 1812 was fought mainly in the northern United States and southern Canada. This map depicts some of the major battles of the War of 1812, which brought few lasting gains to either the United States or Great Britain.

own Cabinet, or to promote officers who had proven themselves in battle.

Because of these problems, permanent changes were made in the administration of the United States military after the war. The army and navy were strengthened and experienced aides were assigned to secretaries of war to ensure that the standing army and navy were well trained and ready in time of need.

A Victory at Ghent

In the peace negotiations at Ghent, Belgium, however, the United States' record was much better. At the table the American delegates consistently outmaneuvered the British and achieved a victory because of what they avoided losing.

John Quincy Adams and his associates took a firm stand from the beginning. They flatly refused to discuss the first British demands made on August 8, 1814: the "retention of conquered territory," the return of lands in the old Northwest to the American Indians, and the right to navigate the Mississippi River.[1]

In the final negotiated version, the British gave up on all these issues. The Treaty of Ghent ordered all conquered lands returned. The idea of an Indian state was abandoned, and nothing at all was said about Mississippi River navigation rights. As for the issues that had led to war, impressment and maritime right of neutral countries, they were also completely ignored.

Though the American delegates had managed to do exactly what they had been instructed to do—negotiate a return to the way things had been before the war—they were nervous about the treaty's reception in the United States.[2] However, Americans viewed the Battle of New Orleans as a victorious end to the war, and nobody cared much about the details of the peace treaty now that the war was over.[3]

Change for the Good

Gallatin, one of the delegates at Ghent, later said that "[t]he war has been productive of evil and good, but I think that the good preponderates [is greater]. . . ."[4]

One positive change was the respect that the United States earned from countries in Europe. Even though the American forces had suffered many defeats, the United States Navy's victories at sea helped build this new admiration.

American manufacturing benefited from the embargo, non-intercourse, and the war itself. War increased the demand for manufactured products, but also made it impossible to import enough goods. The United States, in fact, was cut off from Great Britain, its main supplier of factory-made products. The result was an industrial explosion in the United States that, in time of peace, would probably have taken twenty years.

The real losers in the War of 1812 were the American Indians. Tecumseh's confederacy was the last serious attempt to unite the tribes to resist the white settlers over-running their hunting grounds. In the summer of 1815, the United States signed treaties with the fifteen tribes who had fought alongside the British. In these treaties, the

One of the American delegates at Ghent was Gallatin, who believed that the outcome of the war had been good for the American spirit.

American Indians were promised all the territories they controlled in 1811. However, not one acre of land was ever returned to them. In addition to not giving up these Indian lands, the United States also retained control of part of the Spanish territory of West Florida that had been seized in 1813 as part of Jackson's preparations to protect the Gulf coast of the United States from British invasion.

Finally, the war renewed feelings of national pride that had originally inspired the thirteen American colonies to fight for their independence from Great Britain. Gallatin summed it up: "They [the citizens] are more American; they feel and act more as a nation, and I hope that permanency of the Union is thereby secured."[5]

Poets, Heroes, and Politics

Francis Scott Key, inspired by patriotism when he saw Fort McHenry's American flag still flying after the British siege, penned a poem. He is remembered today as the author of the American national anthem, "The Star-Spangled Banner."

Many others, recognized as American heroes during the war, were later elected to important government positions. John Quincy Adams served as secretary of state under President James Monroe. Then in 1824, Adams became the sixth president of the United States.

Henry Clay continued as the Speaker of the House of Representatives after the war, then was elected to the Senate in 1831. Clay and General Andrew Jackson faced off in the presidential election of 1832. Jackson won and completed two terms.

William Henry Harrison entered Congress in 1816 and later became a senator. In 1840, he defeated Henry Clay for the presidency. Harrison's military record and his slogan "Tippecanoe and Tyler, too" won him a landslide victory. One month after his inauguration, Harrison died of pneumonia. His vice president, John Tyler, became the tenth president of the United States.

Even First Lady Dolley Madison earned a place in history for her coolheadedness during battle. The story of her determined efforts to save a piece of American history, George Washington's portrait, makes her one of the United States' most famous first ladies.

National Memories Preserved

The War of 1812 has sometimes been called the forgotten war. However, even today visitors can step back through time and visit places where many of the important events took place.

In Battle Ground, Indiana, a museum sits near the Tippecanoe Battlefield, where William Henry Harrison defeated the Shawnee warriors led by The Prophet. The site of the Raisin River Massacre is preserved near Monroe, Michigan. Visitors can also walk the battlefield where Andrew Jackson defeated the British and learn more about the famous pirate Jean Lafitte at the Chalmette National Historical Park in New Orleans, Louisiana.

The Sackets Harbor Battlefield and Navy Yard Restoration State Historic Site in New York State features two museums. Displays inside the Commandant's House and in the 1812 Navy Exhibit tell about the history of the town and its part in the war. Oliver Hazard Perry's flagship, the *Niagara*, is located at Erie, Pennsylvania, and a memorial to his victory on Lake Erie stands in Put-in-Bay, Ohio (near Sandusky). The U.S.S. *Constitution*, now docked in Boston Harbor, is a popular attraction. Visitors can walk the decks while marines, dressed in naval uniforms of the early 1800s, tell tales of the ship's colorful past.

Visitors to the U.S.S. *Constitution*, now docked in Boston Harbor, can walk the decks with Marines dressed in naval uniforms of the early 1800s.

The American flag still waves over Baltimore's Fort McHenry, which has been restored and is open to visitors.

In Perrysburg, Ohio, Fort Meigs has been reconstructed on its original site. Exhibits about the history of the area and its role in the War of 1812 are displayed in seven blockhouses on the fort grounds. Our country's flag still waves twenty-four hours a day over Baltimore's Fort McHenry. The star-shaped fort has been restored and is open to visitors. The star-spangled banner that Key saw on the morning of September 14, 1814, is now on display at the Smithsonian Institute in Washington, D.C.

The End at Last

One author called this conflict "the war nobody won."[6] However, having won the last battle, the Americans were convinced that they won the War of 1812. The Canadians, having stopped the American invasion, believed that they had won the war. And the British, having given up nothing that they considered important, were also convinced that they had won.

Perhaps the phrase that best describes this time in the history of the United States is "the incredible War of 1812."[7] From beginning to end, with all its twists and turns, this early chapter in American history is full of interesting events and characters that helped make the United States what it is today.

Timeline

1806—Great Britain proclaims a blockade of the European coast; Napoleon blockades the British Isles.

1807—Jefferson recommends and Congress passes the Embargo Act of 1807; British Royal Navy fires on the U.S.S. *Chesapeake* on June 22.

1809—James Madison inaugurated on March 4; Embargo Act is repealed and replaced by the Non-Intercourse Act in March.

1811—The Prophet defeated by William Henry Harrison on November 7 at Battle of Tippecanoe.

1812—Madison signs War Bill on June 18; Great Britain captures Fort Michilimackinac on July 17; Fort Dearborn massacre on August 15; General Henry Dearborn surrenders to the British at Detroit on August 16; Battle of Queenston fought on October 13; United States Army retreats from eastern Canada by November 23.

1813—Battle of Frenchtown on January 22; Raisin River Massacre on January 23; Battle of York fought on April 27; Battle of Fort George on May 27; Battle of Sackets Harbor on May 29; Battle of Lake Erie on September 10; Battle of the Thames on October 5; Great Britain offers to begin peace negotiations with the United States on November 4; United States adopts embargo on December 17.

1814—Napoleon relinquishes the throne on April 11; United States repeals the Embargo Act; Peace negotiations begin in Ghent on August 8; Battle of Bladensburg on August 25; British burn Washington on August 24–25; Battle of Baltimore fought on September 13–14; Francis Scott Key writes the "Star-Spangled Banner" on September 14; Battle of Lake Borgne on December 14; Skirmishes around New Orleans from December 23–January 15, 1815; United States and Great Britain sign the Treaty of Ghent on December 24.

1815—Battle of New Orleans on January 8; Treaty of Ghent reaches the United States on February 11; United States Senate approves the treaty on February 16 and Madison signs; United States and Great Britain exchange ratifications ending the War of 1812 on February 17.

Chapter Notes

Chapter 1. "Old Hickory" and the Battle of New Orleans

1. Samuel Carter III, *Blaze of Glory, the Fight for New Orleans, 1814-1815* (New York: St. Martin's Press, 1971), p. 104.
2. Ibid.
3. Ibid.
4. Albert Marrin, *1812: The War Nobody Won* (New York: Atheneum, 1985), p. 151.
5. Robin Reilly, *The British at the Gates, the New Orleans Campaign in the War of 1812* (New York: G.P. Putnam's Sons, 1974), p. 242.
6. Donald R. Hickey, *The War of 1812: A Forgotten Conflict* (Urbana: University of Illinois Press, 1989), p. 209.
7. Ibid., p. 212.
8. Ibid.
9. Ibid.

Chapter 2. The Brink of War

1. Harry L. Coles, *The War of 1812* (Chicago: University of Chicago Press, 1965), p. 4.
2. Ibid., p. 7.
3. Donald R. Hickey, *The War of 1812: A Forgotten Conflict* (Urbana: University of Illinois Press, 1989), p. 25.

Chapter 3. Disaster at Fort Detroit

1. Pierre Berton, *The Invasion of Canada 1812–1813* (Toronto: McClelland and Steward, 1980), p. 123.
2. Harry L. Coles, *The War of 1812* (Chicago: University of Chicago Press, 1965), p. 52.
3. Ibid., p. 53.
4. Donald R. Hickey, *The War of 1812: A Forgotten Conflict* (Urbana: University of Illinois Press, 1989), p. 84.
5. Berton, p. 99.

Chapter 4. "Don't Give Up the Ship"
1. Harry L. Coles, *The War of 1812* (Chicago: University of Chicago Press, 1965), p. 80.
2. Donald R. Hickey, *The War of 1812: A Forgotten Conflict* (Urbana: University of Illinois Press, 1989), p. 94.
3. Ibid.
4. Coles, p. 87.
5. Hickey, p. 96.
6. John K. Mahon, *The War of 1812* (Gainesville: The University of Florida Press, 1972), p. 123.
7. Ibid., pp. 124–125.

Chapter 5. In the Northwest Territory
1. Harry L. Coles, *The War of 1812* (Chicago: University of Chicago Press, 1965), p. 113.
2. Ibid., p. 119.
3. Ibid., p. 121.
4. Donald R. Hickey, *The War of 1812: A Forgotten Conflict* (Urbana: University of Illinois Press, 1989), p. 137.

Chapter 6. Battle for the Great Lakes
1. Harry L. Coles, *The War of 1812* (Chicago: University of Chicago Press, 1965), p. 108.
2. Donald R. Hickey, *The War of 1812: A Forgotten Conflict* (Urbana: University of Illinois Press, 1989), p. 130.
3. Coles, p. 124.
4. Ibid., p. 129.

Chapter 7. The Country's Capital Captured
1. Harry L. Coles, *The War of 1812* (Chicago: University of Chicago Press, 1965), p. 151.
2. Pierre Berton, *Flames Across the Border* (Boston: Little, Brown and Company, 1981), p. 367.
3. Ibid., p. 366.
4. Kate Caffrey, *The Twilight's Last Gleaming: Britain vs. America 1812–1815* (New York: Stein and Day, 1977), p. 238.

5. Ibid.
6. Ibid., p. 239.
7. Ibid., p. 247.

Chapter 8. Winning the Peace Talks

1. Donald R. Hickey, *The War of 1812: A Forgotten Conflict* (Urbana: University of Illinois Press, 1989), p. 282.
2. Ibid., p. 287.
3. J. Mackey Hitsman, *The Incredible War of 1812* (Toronto: University of Toronto Press, 1965), p. 232.
4. Pierre Berton, *Flames Across the Border* (Boston: Little, Brown and Company, 1981), p. 407.
5. Ibid.
6. John K. Mahon, *The War of 1812* (Gainesville: The University of Florida Press, 1972), p. 381.

Chapter 9. Lasting Effects of the War of 1812

1. J. Mackey Hitsman, *The Incredible War of 1812* (Toronto: University of Toronto Press, 1965), p. 232.
2. Pierre Berton, *Flames Across the Border* (Boston: Little, Brown and Company, 1981), p. 424.
3. Ibid.
4. John K. Mahon, *The War of 1812* (Gainesville: The University of Florida Press, 1972), p. 384.
5. Ibid.
6. Albert Marrin, *1812: The War Nobody Won* (New York: Atheneum, 1985), title page.
7. Hitsman, title page.

Further Reading

Books

Connell, Kate. *These Lands Are Ours: Tecumseh's Fight for the Old Northwest*. Chatham, N.J.: Raintree Steck-Vaughn, 1993.

Fitz-Gerald, Christine Maloney. *William Henry Harrison: Ninth President of the United States*. Danbury, Conn.: Children's Press, 1987.

Gay, Kathlyn and Martin K. Gay. *The War of 1812*. Brookfield, Conn.: Twentyfirst Century Books, 1995.

Greenblatt, Miriam. *The War of 1812*. New York: Facts on File, Inc., 1994.

Judson, Karen. *Andrew Jackson*. Springfield, N.J.: Enslow Publishers, Inc., 1997.

King, David C. *New Orleans: Battlefields Across America*. Brookfield, Conn.: Millbrook Press, 1998.

Malone, Mary. *James Madison*. Springfield, N.J.: Enslow Publishers, Inc., 1997.

Pflueger, Lynda. *Dolley Madison: Courageous First Lady*. Springfield, N.J.: Enslow Publishers, Inc., 1999.

Internet Addresses

Smithsonian Institution. "Star-Spangled Banner and the War of 1812." © 1995–2001.
<http://www.si.edu/resource/faq/nmah/starflag.htm>

Thinkquest Team #22916. "Re-living History: The War of 1812." Thinkquest. © 1998.
<http://library.thinkquest.org/22916/exmain.html>

"The War of 1812 Homepage." The Napoleonic Wargame Pages. n.d.
<http://warof1812.napoleoicwars.com>

Index